R Programming
100 Interview Questions

X.Y. Wang

Contents

1 Introduction   5

2 Basic   7

    2.1   What is R programming language and what are its primary uses? 7

    2.2   How do you install packages in R? Give an example. 8

    2.3   Explain the difference between a vector and a list in R. 10

    2.4   How do you create a data frame in R? 11

    2.5   What are the basic data types in R? Provide examples. 13

    2.6   What is the purpose of the c() function in R? . 14

    2.7   What are R's control structures, such as loops and conditional statements? 16

2.8   What is the difference between lapply and sapply functions in R? 18

2.9   How can you handle missing values in R? . . . 20

2.10 What are the basic operations you can perform on a matrix in R? 22

2.11 How do you read and write data from/to a CSV file in R? 25

2.12 What is the purpose of the "na.rm" argument in certain functions, such as mean() and sum()? 27

2.13 What are factors in R and why are they useful? 28

2.14 How do you subset data in R using square brackets []? 30

2.15 Explain the difference between a function and a script in R. 32

2.16 What is the purpose of the "..." (ellipsis) argument in R functions? 34

2.17 What is the difference between the assignment operators "<-" and "=" in R? 35

2.18 How do you generate random numbers in R? . . 37

2.19 What are some common R programming errors and how can you debug them? 38

2.20 Explain the concept of a workspace in R and how to save and load it. 40

3 Intermediate   43

3.1   What is the difference between R base and tidy-
       verse packages? Provide examples of some pop-
       ular tidyverse packages. 43

3.2   How do you merge two data frames in R? Ex-
       plain the different types of joins. 45

3.3   What is the concept of "tidy data" and how does
       it relate to R programming? 47

3.4   Explain the apply() function in R and provide
       an example of its usage. 49

3.5   What is the difference between deep and shallow
       copies of objects in R? How do you create each
       type of copy? 51

3.6   How do you handle and import data from Excel
       files in R? 53

3.7   Describe the split-apply-combine strategy in R
       and provide an example using the aggregate()
       function. 54

3.8   Explain the concept of "vectorization" in R and
       why it is important. 55

3.9   What is the difference between rbind() and cbind()
       functions in R? Provide examples. 57

3.10   How do you create a custom R function? Ex-
       plain the structure and syntax. 58

3.11 What is a package namespace in R? Why is it important? 60

3.12 What are anonymous functions in R and how do you create one? 61

3.13 Explain the concept of "lazy evaluation" in R and provide an example. 63

3.14 What is the difference between seq() and rep() functions in R? Provide examples. 64

3.15 How do you use regular expressions in R for pattern matching and text manipulation? 65

3.16 Describe the concepts of "scope" and "environments" in R and how they impact variable visibility. 67

3.17 What is the purpose of the str() function in R and how is it useful for data exploration? 69

3.18 How do you visualize data in R using base graphics and ggplot2? 70

3.19 Explain the concept of "recycling" in R and provide an example. 72

3.20 How do you handle date and time objects in R? Provide examples using the lubridate package. . 74

4 Advanced 77

4.1   How do you optimize R code for performance? Provide examples of profiling tools and techniques. 77

4.2   What is the concept of "parallel computing" in R? Explain how to use the parallel package for parallel processing. 80

4.3   Explain the difference between S3 and S4 object systems in R. Provide examples of their usage. . 82

4.4   Describe the concept of "functional programming" in R and its advantages. Provide examples using the purrr package. 84

4.5   How do you create interactive web applications using R? Explain the role of the Shiny package. 85

4.6   Describe the use of the RMarkdown package for creating reproducible reports in R. 87

4.7   Explain the concept of "memoization" in R and how it can be used to optimize function calls. . 89

4.8   How do you connect to and work with databases in R? Provide examples using the DBI package. 90

4.9   What is the role of unit testing in R programming? Explain the use of the testthat package. . 92

4.10 Describe how to work with API endpoints in R using the httr package. 93

4.11 How do you handle large datasets in R, both in memory and on disk? Provide examples using the data.table and ff packages. 95

4.12 Explain the concept of "web scraping" in R and provide examples using the rvest package. . . . 97

4.13 How do you create custom ggplot2 themes and geoms for data visualization in R? 98

4.14 Describe the use of the foreach package for parallel and sequential iterations in R. 100

4.15 What is the role of cross-validation in machine learning and how do you implement it in R? . . 102

4.16 Explain the use of the caret package for creating and evaluating predictive models in R. 104

4.17 How do you perform text mining and natural language processing in R? Provide examples using the tm and tidytext packages. 106

4.18 Describe the concept of "time series analysis" in R and provide examples using the xts and forecast packages. 107

4.19 What is the role of the devtools package in R package development? Explain its main features. 109

4.20 How do you create and customize R package documentation using the roxygen2 package? . . 111

5 Expert 113

5.1   Explain the process of creating and submitting
      a package to CRAN, including the steps involved
      and requirements to meet. 113

5.2   How do you implement object-oriented program-
      ming in R using both S4 and R6 systems? Pro-
      vide examples. 115

5.3   Describe best practices for managing dependen-
      cies and version control in R projects. 118

5.4   Explain the role of Continuous Integration (CI)
      and Continuous Deployment (CD) in R package
      development. Provide examples using tools such
      as GitHub Actions and Travis CI. 120

5.5   How do you manage large-scale R projects with
      multiple contributors? Discuss tools and prac-
      tices for collaboration and organization. 123

5.6   Describe methods for handling and analyzing
      spatial data in R, including packages such as sf
      and sp. 125

5.7   Explain advanced techniques for parallel and
      distributed computing in R, such as using the
      future and rhipe packages. 127

5.8   How do you develop custom algorithms for high-
      performance computing in R? Discuss using Rcpp
      for C++ integration. 129

5.9   Describe methods for handling and analyzing
      network data in R, including packages such as
      igraph and network. 131

5.10 Explain advanced statistical modeling techniques in R, such as Bayesian modeling and hierarchical models, using packages like rstan and brms.   . . 134

5.11 How do you implement advanced machine learning techniques in R, including deep learning and reinforcement learning? Provide examples using packages like keras and reinforcementlearning.   . 136

5.12 Discuss advanced time series analysis techniques in R, such as state-space models and dynamic factor models, using packages like KFAS and dynfactor. 138

5.13 Explain the process of deploying R-based solutions in production environments, including best practices and challenges. 140

5.14 How do you create custom Shiny components and extend the functionality of existing Shiny widgets? 142

5.15 Describe advanced techniques for data visualization in R, such as interactive and 3D visualizations, using packages like plotly and rayshader.   144

5.16 Explain the use of Docker for creating reproducible and portable R environments. 146

5.17 How do you ensure the security and privacy of sensitive data when working with R projects? Discuss best practices and tools. 148

5.18 Discuss advanced text mining techniques in R, such as topic modeling and sentiment analysis, using packages like stm and syuzhet. 150

5.19 Explain advanced techniques for working with API endpoints in R, including authentication and rate limiting, using packages like httr and rate-limiter. 152

5.20 Describe methods for integrating R with other programming languages and platforms, such as Python and Spark, using packages like reticulate and sparklyr. 154

6 Guru   **157**

6.1 Discuss the role of R in the broader landscape of data science and statistical programming languages. Compare and contrast R with other languages like Python and Julia. 157

6.2 Explain how to design and implement custom domain-specific languages (DSLs) in R for specialized use cases. 158

6.3 Describe the challenges and best practices for scaling R-based solutions in large organizations and complex systems. 160

6.4 Discuss advanced statistical theory and its application in R, including topics such as asymptotic analysis, non-parametric methods, and causal inference. 163

6.5   Explain how to develop and maintain high-quality, performant, and stable R packages that address the needs of a specific domain or industry.   . . . 164

6.6   Describe the role of R in the development of cutting-edge algorithms and models in fields such as artificial intelligence, network science, and bioinformatics.   167

6.7   Discuss the state-of-the-art in R-based data visualization, including innovative techniques and research in the field. 169

6.8   Explain the use of R in the development of advanced statistical models for social science, economics, and public policy.   171

6.9   Describe the role of R in the analysis and modeling of complex systems, such as ecological, financial, or transportation systems.   172

6.10 Discuss the use of R in the development of advanced machine learning models for image, audio, and video processing. 174

6.11 Explain the role of R in addressing ethical and social implications of data science, such as fairness, accountability, and transparency in algorithm design and deployment.   176

6.12 Describe the use of R in the development of custom tools for data-driven decision-making and optimization in specific industries or domains.   . 177

6.13 Discuss the role of R in the analysis of large-scale, high-dimensional, and streaming data, including the development of advanced algorithms and models for big data. 179

6.14 Explain the use of R in addressing the challenges of reproducibility, provenance, and data management in data science. 181

6.15 Describe the role of R in the development of advanced tools and platforms for data collaboration, data sharing, and data publishing. 182

6.16 Discuss the use of R in the analysis and modeling of complex networks, such as social networks, biological networks, and the World Wide Web. . 184

6.17 Explain the role of R in the development of advanced models for natural language processing, text mining, and computational linguistics. . . . 185

6.18 Describe the use of R in the development of advanced techniques for data integration, data cleaning, and data transformation. 188

6.19 Discuss the role of R in the development of cutting-edge techniques for data privacy and security, such as differential privacy and secure multi-party computation. 189

6.20 Explain the use of R in the development of advanced tools and platforms for data education, data literacy, and data communication. 191

Chapter 1

Introduction

Welcome to "R Programming: 100 Interview Questions", an essential resource for anyone looking to advance their knowledge and skills in R programming. This book is designed to help you prepare for interviews or simply deepen your understanding of the R programming language, which has become a popular tool for data analysis, visualization, and statistical modeling.

The book is divided into five main sections, each corresponding to a different level of R proficiency: Basic, Intermediate, Advanced, Expert, and Guru. Each section covers a range of topics and questions that you may encounter in an interview or while working on real-world projects.

In the Basic section, you will learn about the fundamentals of R programming, such as data types, control structures, and basic data manipulation techniques. This section provides a solid foundation for those new to R or looking to brush up on the basics.

The Intermediate section delves deeper into the world of R, exploring topics like the tidyverse, the apply() function, and working with Excel files. As you progress through this section, you will become more comfortable with the language and its various packages, allowing you to tackle more complex tasks.

The Advanced section builds upon the previous sections, introducing concepts like parallel computing, object-oriented programming, and web scraping. You will also learn about advanced data visualization techniques and how to connect to databases in R.

In the Expert section, you will be exposed to topics like creating and submitting a package to CRAN, implementing object-oriented programming with S4 and R6 systems, and managing dependencies and version control. This section will help you further sharpen your skills and prepare for high-level roles in R programming.

Finally, the Guru section focuses on the broader landscape of data science, discussing the role of R in comparison to other programming languages like Python and Julia. You will also learn about advanced techniques in specific domains, such as artificial intelligence, network science, and bioinformatics.

As you work through "R Programming 100 Interview Questions," you will gain a comprehensive understanding of R programming, positioning yourself for success in interviews and professional endeavors alike. Whether you're a novice looking to get started with R or an experienced user seeking to expand your knowledge, this book will provide valuable insights and guidance.

Chapter 2

Basic

2.1 What is R programming language and what are its primary uses?

R is a programming language and software environment for statistical computing and graphics. It was developed by statisticians for statisticians, with a focus on data analysis, data visualization, and statistical modeling. R is an open-source programming language, meaning it is freely available to use and can be modified and distributed by anyone.

One of the primary uses of R is data analysis. R provides a wide range of statistical and graphical techniques for analyzing data, including linear and nonlinear modeling, classical statistical tests, time-series analysis, and clustering. R also provides powerful tools for data manipulation and cleaning, making it a popular choice for data wrangling tasks.

Another primary use of R is data visualization. R provides a variety of graphing and visualization tools, including basic plots, 3D graphs, and interactive visualizations. With packages like ggplot2, users can create publication-quality graphs and customize them to their specific needs.

R is also used for machine learning and predictive modeling. R has a large and growing collection of machine learning packages that provide a variety of algorithms, including decision trees, random forests, support vector machines, and neural networks. R also provides tools for model selection and evaluation, making it a powerful tool for building predictive models.

R is used in a wide range of industries and fields, including finance, healthcare, social sciences, and government. Some specific examples of R's use in these fields include financial risk modeling, genomics research, social network analysis, and political polling.

Overall, R is a powerful tool for data analysis, visualization, and modeling, and its popularity is only continuing to grow as more and more organizations recognize its value.

2.2   How do you install packages in R? Give an example.

To install packages in R, you can use the install.packages() function. This function downloads and installs the specified package and any dependencies it requires.

Here is an example of how to install the ggplot2 package, which is a popular package for creating high-quality data visualizations:

```
install.packages("ggplot2")
```

When you run this code in your R console, R will connect to the Comprehensive R Archive Network (CRAN) and download the ggplot2 package and its dependencies. Depending on your internet speed, this may take a few seconds to a few minutes.

You can also install packages from other sources, such as GitHub or Bioconductor, using different functions or package managers. For example, to install a package from GitHub, you can use the devtools package and the install_github() function:

```
# First, install the devtools package
install.packages("devtools")

# Then install the package from GitHub
devtools::install_github("username/repo")
```

In this example, replace "username/repo" with the actual username and repository name of the package you want to install.

Once a package is installed, you can load it into your R session using the library() function. For example, to load the ggplot2 package, you would run:

```
library(ggplot2)
```

This makes the functions and data sets in the ggplot2 package available for use in your R code.

2.3   Explain the difference between a vector and a list in R.

In R, a vector is an ordered collection of elements of the same data type, while a list is an ordered collection of elements that can be of different data types.

Vectors in R can be created using the c() function, which combines values into a single vector. For example:

```
# Creating a numeric vector
x <- c(1, 2, 3, 4, 5)

# Creating a character vector
y <- c("a", "b", "c")
```

Vectors can also be created using functions like seq() or rep(), which generate sequences or repeated values, respectively.

Lists in R are created using the list() function, which takes any number of arguments and combines them into a list. The elements of a list can be of different data types, and can even be other lists. For example:

```
# Creating a list with numeric and character elements
my_list <- list(1, "a", 3.14)

# Creating a list with a nested list
nested_list <- list("a", "b", list("x", "y"))
```

To access elements of a vector, you can use indexing with square brackets. For example, to get the third element of the vector x, you would write x[3].

To access elements of a list, you can also use indexing with square brackets. However, since lists can contain elements of different types, you may need to use the $ operator to access named elements or the [[ ]] operator to access unnamed elements. For example, to get the second element of my_list, which is a character string, you would write my_list[[2]]. To get the first element of nested_list, which is itself a list, you would write nested_list[[1]].

In summary, the main difference between a vector and a list in R is that vectors contain elements of the same data type, while lists can contain elements of different data types, including other lists. Vectors are indexed with square brackets, while lists may require the $ or [[ ]] operators to access specific elements.

2.4 How do you create a data frame in R?

In R, a data frame is a two-dimensional table-like structure, where each column can have a different data type. Data frames are a common way of representing data in R, especially for statistical analysis.

To create a data frame in R, you can use the data.frame() function. This function takes named arguments, where the names are the column names and the values are vectors containing the data for each column. Here's an example:

```
# Creating a data frame
df <- data.frame(
    name = c("Alice", "Bob", "Charlie"),
    age = c(25, 30, 35),
    height = c(1.6, 1.8, 1.7),
    married = c(TRUE, TRUE, FALSE)
)

# Displaying the data frame
```

```
df
```

In this example, we've created a data frame with four columns: "name", "age", "height", and "married". The "name" column contains character strings, the "age" column contains numeric values, the "height" column contains numeric values with decimal places, and the "married" column contains logical values (TRUE or FALSE).

You can also add a new column to an existing data frame by assigning a vector to a new column name. For example, to add a "weight" column to the df data frame, you can write:

```
df$weight <- c(60, 80, 70)
```

This creates a new column named "weight" and assigns it the vector c(60, 80, 70).

Once you've created a data frame, you can perform operations on it using built-in functions like summary(), which provides a summary of the columns, or subset(), which creates a subset of the data frame based on specified criteria.

In summary, a data frame is a two-dimensional table-like structure in R that can contain columns of different data types. You can create a data frame using the data.frame() function, and you can add new columns using indexing with the $ operator.

2.5 What are the basic data types in R? Provide examples.

R has several basic data types, including numeric, character, logical, integer, complex, and raw.

Numeric: Numeric data types represent numbers, and can be either integers or real numbers. In R, numeric data types are represented by the numeric class. For example:

```
# Creating a numeric variable
x <- 3.14
class(x) # numeric
```

Character: Character data types represent text, and are represented by the character class in R. Character strings are surrounded by either single or double quotes. For example:

```
# Creating a character variable
y <- "hello"
class(y) # character
```

Logical: Logical data types represent boolean values (TRUE or FALSE), and are represented by the logical class in R. For example:

```
# Creating a logical variable
z <- TRUE
class(z) # logical
```

Integer: Integer data types represent whole numbers, and are represented by the integer class in R. In contrast to numeric data types, integer data types cannot have decimal points. For example: r Copy code # Creating an integer variable a <- 5L class(a) # integer

Note that the L at the end of 5L indicates that a is an integer.

Complex: Complex data types represent complex numbers, and are represented by the complex class in R. Complex numbers have both a real and imaginary component. For example:

```
# Creating a complex variable
b <- 3 + 2i
class(b) # complex
```

Raw: Raw data types represent raw bytes, and are represented by the raw class in R. Raw data can be used to represent binary data, such as images or sound files. For example:

```
# Creating a raw variable
c <- charToRaw("hello")
class(c) # raw
```

In summary, R has several basic data types, including numeric, character, logical, integer, complex, and raw. These data types are represented by different classes in R, and each has its own specific uses and applications.

2.6   What is the purpose of the c() function in R?

In R, the c() function is used to concatenate or combine values into a single vector or list. The c() function stands for "concatenate", and is a basic and frequently used function in R.

The c() function can take any number of arguments, which can be of different data types, and returns a single object of the same data type. For example:

```
# Concatenating numeric values
x <- c(1, 2, 3, 4, 5)

# Concatenating character values
```

```
y <- c("a", "b", "c")

# Concatenating values of different types
z <- c(1, "a", TRUE)
```

In the first example, c(1, 2, 3, 4, 5) creates a numeric vector with the values 1 through 5. In the second example, c("a", "b", "c") creates a character vector with the values "a", "b", and "c". In the third example, c(1, "a", TRUE) creates a vector with three elements of different data types: a numeric value of 1, a character value of "a", and a logical value of TRUE. In this case, R will coerce the numeric and logical values to character values in order to create a single character vector.

The c() function can also be used to combine vectors or lists into a larger vector or list. For example:

```
# Combining two numeric vectors
a <- c(1, 2, 3)
b <- c(4, 5, 6)
c <- c(a, b)

# Combining two lists
list1 <- list("a", 1)
list2 <- list("b", 2)
list3 <- c(list1, list2)
```

In the first example, c(a, b) combines the a and b vectors into a single vector with the values 1 through 6. In the second example, c(list1, list2) combines the list1 and list2 lists into a single list with four elements.

In summary, the c() function in R is used to concatenate or combine values into a single vector or list. It can take any number of arguments of different data types, and returns a single object of the same data type. The c() function is a basic and frequently used function in R, and is an important part of working with vectors and lists.

2.7   What are R's control structures, such as loops and conditional statements?

In R, control structures are used to control the flow of execution in a program. Control structures allow you to execute specific blocks of code under certain conditions or to iterate over a sequence of values. Some of the main control structures in R are loops and conditional statements.

Conditional statements: Conditional statements are used to execute code based on certain conditions. In R, conditional statements are implemented using the if, else if, and else keywords. The basic syntax for an if statement is:

```
if (condition) {
    # code to execute if the condition is TRUE
} else {
    # code to execute if the condition is FALSE
}
```

Here's an example that uses an if statement to check if a number is even or odd:

```
x <- 5

if (x %% 2 == 0) {
    print("x is even")
} else {
    print("x is odd")
}
```

In this example, the % operator returns the remainder of x divided by 2. If the remainder is 0, then x is even, and the first code block is executed. Otherwise, x is odd, and the second code block is executed.

Loops: Loops are used to execute a block of code repeatedly, either a fixed number of times or until a certain condition is met. In R, there are several types of loops, including for loops, while loops, and repeat loops.

The basic syntax for a for loop is:

```
for (variable in sequence) {
    # code to execute for each value of the variable
}
```

Here's an example that uses a for loop to print the numbers from 1 to 5:

```
for (i in 1:5) {
    print(i)
}
```

The basic syntax for a while loop is:

```
while (condition) {
    # code to execute while the condition is TRUE
}
```

Here's an example that uses a while loop to print the numbers from 1 to 5:

```
i <- 1

while (i <= 5) {
    print(i)
    i <- i + 1
}
```

In this example, the loop continues to execute as long as i is less than or equal to 5. The i <- i + 1 statement increments i by 1 for each iteration of the loop.

The basic syntax for a repeat loop is:

```
repeat {
    # code to execute repeatedly
```

```
    if (condition) {
        break
    }
}
```

Here's an example that uses a repeat loop to print the numbers
from 1 to 5:

```
i <- 1

repeat {
    print(i)
    i <- i + 1
    if (i > 5) {
        break
    }
}
```

In this example, the loop continues to execute indefinitely until
the break statement is reached. The if (i > 5) condition checks
if i has reached 5, and if so, the loop is terminated using break.

In summary, R has several control structures, including conditional statements and loops. Conditional statements allow
you to execute code based on certain conditions, while loops
allow you to execute a block of code repeatedly until a certain
condition is met. Understanding and using these control structures effectively is essential for writing efficient and effective R
programs.

2.8   What is the difference between lapply and sapply functions in R?

In R, lapply() and sapply() are two functions that are used to
apply a function to each element of a list or vector. While

both functions have similar functionality, there are some key differences between them.

The lapply() function stands for "list apply". It takes a list as input and applies a function to each element of the list, returning a list as output. The output list has the same length as the input list, and each element of the output list corresponds to the result of applying the function to the corresponding element of the input list. Here's an example:

```
# Creating a list of numbers
my_list <- list(1, 2, 3, 4, 5)

# Applying the square root function to each element of the
    list
result <- lapply(my_list, sqrt)

# Displaying the result
result
```

In this example, the lapply() function applies the sqrt() function to each element of the my_list list, which contains the numbers 1 through 5. The resulting list, result, contains the square roots of each element of my_list.

The sapply() function stands for "simplified apply". It is similar to lapply(), but it tries to simplify the output to a vector or matrix if possible. If the output of the function applied to each element of the input list is a vector of the same length, sapply() will return a matrix with each element of the vector in a separate column. If the output of the function is a scalar value or a vector of different lengths, sapply() will return a vector. Here's an example:

```
# Creating a list of numbers
my_list <- list(1, 2, 3, 4, 5)

# Applying the square root function to each element of the
    list
```

```
result <- sapply(my_list, sqrt)

# Displaying the result
result
```

In this example, the sapply() function applies the sqrt() function to each element of the my_list list, which contains the numbers 1 through 5. Since the output of the sqrt() function is a scalar value for each element of the list, sapply() returns a vector with the square roots of each element of my_list.

The main difference between lapply() and sapply() is that sapply() tries to simplify the output to a vector or matrix if possible, while lapply() always returns a list. This can be useful if you want to apply a function to a list and get a simplified output in some cases, but want to retain the list structure in others.

In summary, lapply() and sapply() are two functions in R that apply a function to each element of a list or vector. The main difference between them is that sapply() tries to simplify the output to a vector or matrix if possible, while lapply() always returns a list.

2.9 How can you handle missing values in R?

In R, missing values are represented by the special value NA. Handling missing values is an important part of data analysis and modeling, and R provides several functions and methods for dealing with missing values.

Checking for missing values: You can check for missing values in a vector or data frame using the is.na() function, which returns a logical vector of the same length as the input vector or data frame, indicating which values are missing. Here's an example:

```
# Creating a vector with missing values
x <- c(1, 2, NA, 4, NA)

# Checking for missing values
is.na(x)
```

In this example, the is.na() function returns a logical vector indicating that the third and fifth elements of x are missing.

Removing missing values: You can remove missing values from a vector or data frame using the na.omit() function, which removes any rows or columns that contain missing values. Here's an example:

```
# Creating a data frame with missing values
df <- data.frame(x = c(1, 2, NA, 4, NA), y = c(NA, 2, 3, NA
    , 5))

# Removing missing values
df_clean <- na.omit(df)

# Displaying the clean data frame
df_clean
```

In this example, the na.omit() function removes the rows of the df data frame that contain missing values, and returns a clean data frame with only the rows that have complete data.

Imputing missing values: Imputing missing values is the process of estimating missing values based on the available data. R provides several functions for imputing missing values, including mean(), median(), and knn.impute().

```
# Creating a vector with missing values
x <- c(1, 2, NA, 4, NA)
```

```
# Imputing missing values with the mean
mean_x <- mean(x, na.rm = TRUE)
x_imputed <- ifelse(is.na(x), mean_x, x)

# Displaying the imputed vector
x_imputed
```

In this example, we impute the missing values in x by replacing them with the mean value of the non-missing values. The ifelse() function replaces each missing value with the mean value, and leaves the non-missing values unchanged.

In summary, handling missing values is an important part of data analysis in R. You can check for missing values using the is.na() function, remove missing values using the na.omit() function, and impute missing values using functions such as mean() or median(). It is important to carefully consider the best approach for handling missing values in your data, as different methods can have different impacts on the analysis or modeling results.

2.10   What are the basic operations you can perform on a matrix in R?

In R, a matrix is a two-dimensional array in which each element has the same data type. Matrices are a useful data structure for organizing and manipulating data, and R provides several operations that can be performed on matrices.

Creating a matrix: You can create a matrix in R using the matrix() function. The matrix() function takes the data to be arranged in the matrix, the number of rows and columns, and other optional arguments such as row and column names. Here's an example:

```
# Creating a 3x3 matrix
m <- matrix(c(1, 2, 3, 4, 5, 6, 7, 8, 9), nrow = 3, ncol =
    3)

# Displaying the matrix
m
```

In this example, the matrix() function creates a 3x3 matrix with the values 1 through 9.

Accessing elements of a matrix: You can access individual elements of a matrix using the square bracket notation. The first index specifies the row, and the second index specifies the column. Here's an example:

```
# Accessing the element in the second row and third column
m[2, 3]
```

In this example, the square brackets [] are used to access the element in the second row and third column of the matrix m.

Performing operations on matrices: R provides several functions for performing mathematical operations on matrices. Some of the basic operations you can perform on a matrix include: Addition: You can add two matrices of the same size element-wise using the + operator.

```
# Adding two matrices
m1 <- matrix(c(1, 2, 3, 4, 5, 6), nrow = 2, ncol = 3)
m2 <- matrix(c(2, 4, 6, 8, 10, 12), nrow = 2, ncol = 3)
m_sum <- m1 + m2

# Displaying the sum matrix
m_sum
```

In this example, we create two 2x3 matrices m1 and m2, and add them element-wise using the + operator to create a new

2x3 matrix m_sum.

Subtraction: You can subtract two matrices of the same size element-wise using the - operator.

```
# Subtracting two matrices
m_diff <- m2 - m1

# Displaying the difference matrix
m_diff
```

In this example, we subtract m1 from m2 element-wise using the - operator to create a new 2x3 matrix m_diff.

Multiplication: You can multiply two matrices using the %*% operator.

```
# Multiplying two matrices
m1 <- matrix(c(1, 2, 3, 4), nrow = 2, ncol = 2)
m2 <- matrix(c(2, 1, 3, 2), nrow = 2, ncol = 2)
m_prod <- m1 %*% m2

# Displaying the product matrix
m_prod
```

In this example, we multiply m1 and m2 using the %*% operator to create a new 2x2 matrix m_prod.

Transposing a matrix: You can transpose a matrix using the t() function, which swaps the rows and columns of the matrix.

```
# Transposing a matrix
m_transpose <- t(m)

# Displaying the transposed matrix
```

2.11   How do you read and write data from/to a CSV file in R?

In R, CSV files are a common data format for storing and exchanging data. Reading and writing data from/to a CSV file is a common task in data analysis and modeling, and R provides several functions for handling CSV files.

Reading data from a CSV file: You can read data from a CSV file in R using the read.csv() function. The read.csv() function takes the name of the CSV file as input, and returns a data frame containing the data in the CSV file. Here's an example:

```
# Reading data from a CSV file
my_data <- read.csv("my_data.csv")

# Displaying the data frame
my_data
```

In this example, the read.csv() function reads the data from the CSV file "my_data.csv" and stores it in a data frame called my_data.

Writing data to a CSV file: You can write data to a CSV file in R using the write.csv() function. The write.csv() function takes the data to be written and the name of the CSV file as input, and writes the data to the specified file. Here's an example:

```
# Writing data to a CSV file
my_data <- data.frame(x = c(1, 2, 3), y = c(4, 5, 6))
write.csv(my_data, file = "my_data.csv", row.names = FALSE)
```

In this example, we create a data frame called my_data containing two columns, and write it to a CSV file called "my_data.csv" using the write.csv() function. The row.names = FALSE argument tells R not to include row names in the CSV file.

Specifying options for reading and writing CSV files: Both the read.csv() and write.csv() functions have several optional arguments that can be used to customize their behavior. Some of the commonly used options include:

- header: Specifies whether the CSV file contains a header row. The default value is TRUE.

- sep: Specifies the field separator character used in the CSV file. The default value is ,.

- colClasses: Specifies the data types of each column in the CSV file. This can be a vector of class names, or a named list where the names are column names and the values are class names.

- na.strings: Specifies the character strings that should be interpreted as missing values. This can be a vector of character strings.

- quote: Specifies the quote character used in the CSV file. The default value is ".

- row.names: Specifies whether row names should be included in the CSV file. The default value is TRUE.

Here's an example that demonstrates how to use some of these options:

```
# Reading data from a CSV file with custom options
my_data <- read.csv("my_data.csv", header = TRUE, sep = ";"
    , colClasses = c("numeric", "factor"))

# Writing data to a CSV file with custom options
write.csv(my_data, file = "my_data.csv", row.names = FALSE,
    quote = "'", na = "")
```

In this example, we use the header, sep, and colClasses options
to specify that the CSV file has a header row, the field separator
is ;, and the first column should be interpreted as numeric and
the second column as a factor. We also use the quote and
na options to specify that single quotes should be used as the
quote character, and that missing values should be represented
as empty strings.

In summary, reading and writing data from/to a CSV file in R
is a common task in data analysis and modeling. R provides
several functions for handling CSV.

2.12   What is the purpose of the "na.rm" argument in certain functions, such as mean() and sum()?

In R, the na.rm argument is used in certain functions, such as
mean() and sum(), to indicate whether missing values should
be removed from the input before the function is applied. The
na.rm argument is a logical value that defaults to FALSE, which
means that missing values are treated as an error and the function returns NA if any missing values are present. However,
if na.rm is set to TRUE, missing values are removed from the
input before the function is applied, and the result is calculated
based only on the non-missing values.

Here's an example that demonstrates the use of the na.rm argument:

```
# Creating a vector with missing values
x <- c(1, 2, NA, 4, NA)

# Calculating the sum with missing values
```

```
sum(x)
# Returns NA

# Calculating the sum without missing values
sum(x, na.rm = TRUE)
# Returns 7

# Calculating the mean with missing values
mean(x)
# Returns NA

# Calculating the mean without missing values
mean(x, na.rm = TRUE)
# Returns 2.333333
```

In this example, we create a vector x that contains missing values, and calculate the sum and mean of x using the sum() and mean() functions. When na.rm is not specified or set to FALSE, the functions return NA because the input contains missing values. However, when na.rm is set to TRUE, the functions remove the missing values before performing the calculation and return the result based only on the non-missing values.

The na.rm argument is useful when working with data that contains missing values, as it allows you to perform calculations based only on the available data. However, it is important to carefully consider the impact of removing missing values on the analysis or modeling results, as it can introduce bias or other errors.

2.13   What are factors in R and why are they useful?

In R, a factor is a categorical variable that can take on a limited set of values. Factors are useful for representing variables such as gender, race, or educational level, where the possible values are discrete and often unordered. Factors are stored as integer codes that correspond to the levels of the factor, and are typically used for modeling or plotting purposes.

Here's an example of creating a factor in R:

```
# Creating a factor
gender <- factor(c("Male", "Female", "Female", "Male", "
    Male"))
```

In this example, we create a factor called gender that has five levels: "Male" and "Female". The values in the input vector are converted to integer codes that correspond to the levels of the factor.

Factors are useful for several reasons:

Memory efficiency: Factors are stored as integers, which can be more memory-efficient than storing the character strings directly. This can be particularly important when working with large datasets or when modeling with many categorical variables.

Ease of modeling: Many modeling functions in R, such as linear regression and logistic regression, require categorical variables to be represented as factors. By converting categorical variables to factors, you can easily include them in models and analyze the impact of the different levels of the variable on the outcome.

Plotting: Factors are often used in plotting functions to create visualizations that display the distribution of categorical variables. For example, you can use the barplot() function to create a bar chart that shows the frequency of each level of a factor.

Here's an example of using a factor in plotting:

```
# Creating a factor and plotting the frequencies
gender <- factor(c("Male", "Female", "Female", "Male", "
    Male"))
barplot(table(gender))
```

In this example, we use the table() function to count the frequency of each level of the gender factor, and then use the barplot() function to create a bar chart that displays the frequencies.

In summary, factors are a useful data structure in R for representing categorical variables. They are memory-efficient, easy to model, and can be used in plotting functions to create visualizations of categorical data.

2.14   How do you subset data in R using square brackets []?

In R, you can subset data using square brackets []. Subsetting is the process of selecting a subset of rows, columns, or elements from a data frame, matrix, or vector. The square brackets can be used to specify one or more indices, which indicate the subset of data to be selected.

Here are some examples of subsetting data using square brackets:

Subsetting a vector:

```
# Creating a vector
x <- c(1, 2, 3, 4, 5)

# Selecting the second element of the vector
x[2]
# Returns 2
```

```
# Selecting the first three elements of the vector
x[1:3]
# Returns c(1, 2, 3)
```

In this example, we create a vector x and use square brackets to select the second element of the vector (x[2]) and the first three elements of the vector (x[1:3]).

Subsetting a matrix:

```
# Creating a matrix
m <- matrix(c(1, 2, 3, 4, 5, 6), nrow = 2, ncol = 3)

# Selecting the element in the second row and third column
m[2, 3]
# Returns 6

# Selecting the first row of the matrix
m[1, ]
# Returns c(1, 3, 5)
```

In this example, we create a matrix m and use square brackets to select the element in the second row and third column (m[2, 3]) and the first row of the matrix (m[1,]).

Subsetting a data frame:

```
# Creating a data frame
df <- data.frame(x = c(1, 2, 3), y = c(4, 5, 6))

# Selecting the value in the first row and second column of
    the data frame
df[1, 2]
# Returns 4

# Selecting the second column of the data frame
df[, 2]
# Returns c(4, 5, 6)

# Selecting rows where the value of x is greater than 1
df[df$x > 1, ]
# Returns a data frame with rows 2 and 3
```

In this example, we create a data frame df and use square brackets to select the value in the first row and second column of the data frame (df[1, 2]), the second column of the data frame (df[, 2]), and the rows where the value of x is greater than 1 (df[df$x > 1,]).

In summary, subsetting data in R using square brackets [] is a powerful and flexible way to select subsets of rows, columns, or elements from a data frame, matrix, or vector.

2.15   Explain the difference between a function and a script in R.

In R, a function is a block of code that performs a specific task and returns a result. Functions are defined using the function() keyword, and can take one or more arguments as input. Functions are designed to be reusable and modular, and can be called from other parts of the code. In contrast, a script is a series of R commands that are executed in order to perform a specific task. Scripts are typically written to automate a series of tasks or to perform a data analysis.

Here's an example of a function in R:

```
# Defining a function
my_function <- function(x, y) {
    z <- x + y
    return(z)
}

# Calling the function
my_function(2, 3)
# Returns 5
```

In this example, we define a function called my_function that takes two arguments, x and y, adds them together, and returns the result as z. We then call the function with the arguments 2 and 3, and the function returns the value 5.

Here's an example of a script in R:

```
# Loading a data file
my_data <- read.csv("my_data.csv")

# Calculating the mean of a variable
mean_variable <- mean(my_data$variable)

# Printing the result
print(mean_variable)
```

In this example, we load a data file using the read.csv() function, calculate the mean of a variable using the mean() function, and print the result using the print() function. This series of commands can be saved as a script and executed in order to perform the specified tasks.

In summary, functions and scripts are both important parts of the R programming language, but they serve different purposes. Functions are reusable blocks of code that perform a specific task and return a result, while scripts are a series of commands that are executed in order to perform a specific task or automate a series of tasks. Functions are designed to be modular and reusable, while scripts are typically written to perform a specific task or analysis.

2.16   What is the purpose of the "..." (ellipsis) argument in R functions?

In R, the ... (ellipsis) argument in a function definition is used to allow for an arbitrary number of additional arguments to be passed to the function. This is useful when you want to create a function that can handle different input formats or configurations without having to explicitly specify all possible arguments. The ... argument is often used in conjunction with the list() function to collect the additional arguments into a list.

Here's an example of a function that uses the ... argument:

```
my_function <- function(x, y, ...) {
    z <- x + y
    for (arg in list(...)) {
        z <- z + arg
    }
    return(z)
}

my_function(2, 3)
# Returns 5

my_function(2, 3, 4)
# Returns 9

my_function(2, 3, 4, 5)
# Returns 14
```

In this example, we define a function called my_function that takes two required arguments (x and y) and an arbitrary number of additional arguments (...). The function calculates the sum of x and y, and then iterates through the list of additional arguments using a for loop, adding each argument to the sum.

When we call my_function(2, 3) with only two arguments, the function returns the sum of x and y (5). When we call my_function(2, 3, 4) with three arguments, the function adds the additional argument (4) to the sum and returns 9. When we call my_function(2, 3, 4, 5) with four arguments, the function adds all four arguments to the sum and returns 14.

In summary, the ... argument in R functions allows for an arbitrary number of additional arguments to be passed to the function, which can be useful when you want to create a flexible and adaptable function that can handle different input formats or configurations. The list() function can be used to collect the additional arguments into a list, which can then be manipulated or iterated through using other R functions.

2.17 What is the difference between the assignment operators "<-" and "=" in R?

In R, there are two assignment operators: <- and =. Although both operators can be used to assign values to variables, there are some differences between them in terms of their syntax and behavior.

The <- operator is the more traditional assignment operator in R. It is used to assign a value to a variable or to update the value of an existing variable. Here's an example:

```
# Assigning a value to a variable using <-
x <- 5
```

In this example, we assign the value 5 to the variable x using the <- operator.

The = operator is an alternative assignment operator that is
also used to assign a value to a variable. However, the = operator has a slightly different syntax and behavior compared to
<-. Here's an example:

```
# Assigning a value to a variable using =
y = 10
```

In this example, we assign the value 10 to the variable y using
the = operator.

The main differences between <- and = are as follows:

Syntax: The <- operator uses a leftward arrow, while the =
operator uses an equals sign. This can affect the readability
and style of the code.

Precedence: The <- operator has higher precedence than =,
which means that it is evaluated before = in expressions. This
can affect the behavior of the code in some cases.

Compatibility: The <- operator is more widely used and accepted in R, and is the preferred assignment operator in many
cases.

In practice, both <- and = can be used to assign values to
variables in R, and the choice between them often comes down
to personal preference or coding style. However, it is important
to be consistent in your use of assignment operators to avoid
confusion or errors in your code.

2.18   How do you generate random numbers in R?

In R, there are several ways to generate random numbers. Random numbers are often used in statistical simulations, Monte Carlo analyses, and other data analysis tasks.

Here are some common functions for generating random numbers in R:

runif(n, min = 0, max = 1): This function generates n random numbers from a uniform distribution between min and max. For example:

```
# Generating 10 random numbers between 0 and 1
runif(10)
# Returns something like: 0.312, 0.453, 0.234, 0.754,
    0.892, 0.187, 0.832, 0.657, 0.523, 0.109
```

rnorm(n, mean = 0, sd = 1): This function generates n random numbers from a normal distribution with mean mean and standard deviation sd. For example:

```
# Generating 10 random numbers from a normal distribution
    with mean 0 and standard deviation 1
rnorm(10)
# Returns something like: -0.134, 0.561, 1.129, -0.809,
    -0.267, -1.702, -0.491, -0.858, 0.224, -0.283
```

sample(x, size, replace = FALSE): This function generates a random sample of size elements from the vector x. If replace = TRUE, elements can be selected more than once. For example:

```
# Generating a random sample of 5 elements from the vector
    1:10
sample(1:10, 5)
# Returns something like: 3, 5, 1, 9, 2
```

rbinom(n, size, prob): This function generates n random numbers from a binomial distribution with size trials and probability
of success prob. For example:

```
# Generating 10 random numbers from a binomial distribution
    with 10 trials and probability of success 0.5
rbinom(10, 10, 0.5)
# Returns something like: 3, 5, 7, 4, 6, 5, 4, 4, 6, 5
```

There are many other functions for generating random numbers in R, including rexp(), rpois(), rcauchy(), and others. The
choice of which function to use depends on the specific needs of
the analysis or simulation.

In summary, R provides several built-in functions for generating random numbers from various probability distributions.
These functions can be useful for simulating data or conducting statistical analyses that require random samples or random
variables.

2.19   What are some common R program-
         ming errors and how can you debug
         them?

Like any programming language, R can generate errors due to
various reasons, such as syntax errors, logic errors, or data type
mismatches. Here are some common types of R programming
errors and ways to debug them:

Syntax errors: Syntax errors occur when the R code violates
the rules of the language. Common syntax errors include missing parentheses or brackets, mismatched quotes, or misspelled
function names. One way to debug syntax errors is to carefully

review the code and look for missing or extraneous symbols or keywords.

Type errors: Type errors occur when the data type of a variable or function argument is incompatible with the expected data type. For example, trying to apply a mathematical function to a character string can result in a type error. One way to debug type errors is to use the class() function to check the data type of variables or arguments.

Logical errors: Logical errors occur when the code does not produce the intended output due to incorrect or incomplete logic. For example, a loop that does not terminate or a conditional statement that always evaluates to FALSE can result in a logical error. One way to debug logical errors is to use the print() function to check intermediate results and verify the logic of the code.

Missing values: Missing values (denoted by NA) can cause errors or produce unexpected results if not properly handled. One way to debug missing value errors is to use the is.na() function to check for missing values and then decide how to handle them, such as by removing them or imputing them with a reasonable value.

Out of memory errors: R may produce out of memory errors when trying to load large data sets or perform computationally intensive tasks. One way to debug out of memory errors is to optimize the code by using efficient algorithms, reducing the size of the data set, or increasing the amount of available memory.

In addition to these common types of errors, R also provides several tools for debugging and error handling, including the tryCatch() function, which allows for custom error handling, and the debug() function, which can be used to step through code and examine variables at different points in the execution.

In summary, debugging R programming errors requires a combination of careful code review, systematic testing, and use of R's built-in tools for error handling and debugging. Understanding the common types of errors and their causes can help make the debugging process more efficient and effective.

2.20   Explain the concept of a workspace in R and how to save and load it.

In R, a workspace is the current working environment that contains all the variables, functions, and other objects that have been defined or loaded during the current R session. The workspace is stored in memory and is cleared when R is closed or restarted.

The concept of a workspace is important because it allows you to save and load your work between R sessions, or to transfer your work to another computer. Here's how to save and load a workspace in R:

Saving a workspace: To save the current workspace to a file, you can use the save.image() function. By default, the function saves all objects in the workspace to a file called .RData in the current working directory. For example: r Copy code # Save the current workspace to a file called "my_workspace.RData" save.image("my_workspace.RData")

You can also specify a different file name or directory using the file argument.

Loading a workspace: To load a previously saved workspace, you can use the load() function. By default, the function loads the objects from the file called .RData in the current working directory. For example:

```
# Load the workspace from the file "my_workspace.RData"
load("my_workspace.RData")
```

This will load all the objects from the saved workspace into the current R session, allowing you to continue working with them.

It's worth noting that some R users prefer not to use workspaces, as they can lead to confusion or unexpected results if the contents of the workspace are not well understood or properly managed. Instead, many users prefer to explicitly load and save individual data sets or functions using functions like read.csv(), write.csv(), or saveRDS(), which can offer more control over the data being loaded or saved.

In summary, a workspace in R is the current working environment that contains all the objects and functions defined or loaded during an R session. You can save and load a workspace using the save.image() and load() functions, respectively, although it's worth being mindful of the potential pitfalls of using workspaces and exploring alternative methods for managing data and functions between R sessions.

Chapter 3

Intermediate

3.1 What is the difference between R base and tidyverse packages? Provide examples of some popular tidyverse packages.

R is a language that comes with a base set of functions and packages for data manipulation, statistical analysis, and visualization. In addition to the base packages, there are many additional packages available in the R ecosystem that can extend R's capabilities and provide additional functionality.

The tidyverse is a collection of packages that are designed to work together and provide a consistent and efficient approach to data manipulation, exploration, and visualization. The tidyverse packages emphasize a "tidy data" philosophy, which involves organizing data into a consistent format that makes it easier to analyze and visualize.

Here are some key differences between R base and tidyverse packages:

Data manipulation: R base provides some basic functions for data manipulation, such as subset(), merge(), and aggregate(). However, these functions can be verbose and difficult to use for more complex tasks. The tidyverse provides a suite of functions for data manipulation that are designed to be easy to use and read, such as dplyr::filter(), dplyr::mutate(), and tidyr::gather(). These functions allow for complex data manipulations with fewer lines of code.

Visualization: R base provides some basic functions for visualization, such as plot() and hist(). However, these functions can be limited in their flexibility and customization. The tidyverse provides a suite of visualization packages, such as ggplot2 and gganimate, which offer a highly customizable and elegant approach to data visualization.

Syntax: R base and tidyverse packages have different syntax conventions. R base often uses functions that take many arguments, while tidyverse packages use functions that take a single data argument and then use pipes (%>%) to chain together multiple operations. This results in more readable and expressive code in the tidyverse.

Here are some popular tidyverse packages and their main functions:

- ggplot2: A package for creating customizable and aesthetically pleasing visualizations, such as scatter plots, histograms, and bar charts.

- dplyr: A package for data manipulation that provides functions for filtering, selecting, mutating, and summarizing data.

- tidyr: A package for data manipulation that provides functions for reshaping data between wide and long formats.

- purrr: A package for functional programming that provides functions for iterating over lists and data frames.

- stringr: A package for string manipulation that provides functions for pattern matching, substitution, and splitting strings.

In summary, the tidyverse is a collection of packages that provides a modern and powerful approach to data manipulation and visualization in R. While R base provides some basic functionality for data manipulation and visualization, the tidyverse packages offer a more consistent and expressive approach that can make data analysis and visualization faster and more enjoyable.

3.2 How do you merge two data frames in R? Explain the different types of joins.

In R, merging two data frames involves combining them into a single data frame based on a shared key or column. The merge() function is used for merging data frames in R. Here's an example of how to merge two data frames in R:

```
# Create two data frames
df1 <- data.frame(id = c(1, 2, 3), name = c("John", "Mary",
    "Bob"))
df2 <- data.frame(id = c(2, 3, 4), age = c(25, 30, 35))

# Merge the two data frames based on the "id" column
merged_df <- merge(df1, df2, by = "id")
```

This code will create two data frames (df1 and df2) and merge them into a single data frame (merged_df) based on the shared "id" column. The resulting data frame will have columns for "id", "name", and "age".

There are several types of joins that can be used when merging data frames in R:

Inner join: An inner join returns only the rows that have matching values in both data frames. This is the default join type in merge(). For example:

```
merged_df_inner <- merge(df1, df2, by = "id")
```

Left join: A left join returns all the rows from the first (left) data frame and matching rows from the second (right) data frame. For example:

```
merged_df_left <- merge(df1, df2, by = "id", all.x = TRUE)
```

Right join: A right join returns all the rows from the second (right) data frame and matching rows from the first (left) data frame. For example:

```
merged_df_right <- merge(df1, df2, by = "id", all.y = TRUE)
```

Full join: A full join returns all the rows from both data frames, and fills in missing values with NA where there are no matches. For example:

```
merged_df_full <- merge(df1, df2, by = "id", all = TRUE)
```

It's important to note that when merging data frames, the order of the arguments in the merge() function matters. The first argument is the left data frame, and the second argument is the right data frame. The by argument specifies the column(s) to use for the join.

In summary, merging data frames in R involves combining them into a single data frame based on a shared key or column using the merge() function. Different types of joins (inner, left, right, and full) can be used to control how the merge is performed and which rows are included in the resulting data frame.

3.3 What is the concept of "tidy data" and how does it relate to R programming?

The concept of "tidy data" is an important principle in data science that refers to organizing data in a consistent and structured format that makes it easy to analyze and visualize. Tidy data typically follows three main principles:

Each variable forms a column: Each variable in the data set should be represented by a separate column.

Each observation forms a row: Each observation (or data point) in the data set should be represented by a separate row.

Each type of observational unit forms a table: Each data set should correspond to a single observational unit (e.g., a single experiment or study) and be organized into a separate table.

By organizing data in this way, it becomes much easier to manipulate, summarize, and visualize the data using R programming and other data analysis tools. For example, tidy data can
be easily analyzed using the dplyr and ggplot2 packages in the
tidyverse, which are designed to work with tidy data.

Here's an example of how to convert non-tidy data into tidy
data using R:

```
# Create a non-tidy data set
non_tidy_data <- data.frame(
id = c(1, 2, 3),
name = c("John", "Mary", "Bob"),
age_2019 = c(25, 30, 35),
age_2020 = c(26, 31, 36)
)

# Convert the non-tidy data to tidy data
tidy_data <- tidyr::pivot_longer(
non_tidy_data,
cols = starts_with("age"),
names_to = "year",
values_to = "age"
)

# Print the tidy data
print(tidy_data)
```

In this example, we start with a non-tidy data set that contains
columns for "id", "name", "age_2019", and "age_2020". We
then use the tidyr::pivot_longer() function to convert the data
into tidy format by pivoting the "age" columns into a single
column called "age" and creating a new column called "year"
to indicate the year of the age value. The resulting tidy data set
has three columns for "id", "name", and "age", with multiple
rows for each individual corresponding to each year of age data.

In summary, the concept of "tidy data" is a principle of data organization that involves structuring data in a consistent and standardized way to make it easier to analyze and visualize. R programming has a strong emphasis on tidy data, with many packages and tools designed to work with tidy data sets. By following the principles of tidy data, data scientists and analysts can more easily manipulate and analyze data, leading to faster and more accurate insights.

3.4 Explain the apply() function in R and provide an example of its usage.

The apply() function is a powerful and flexible tool for applying a function to a data set in R. It is part of the base R package and can be used with any type of R object that can be treated as a matrix or array, such as data frames, matrices, or lists.

The apply() function takes three arguments: the data object, the margin along which to apply the function (either rows or columns), and the function to apply. Here is the general syntax for using apply():

```
apply(data, margin, function)
```

Here's an example of how to use the apply() function to calculate the mean of each column in a matrix:

```
# Create a matrix
m <- matrix(c(1, 2, 3, 4, 5, 6), ncol = 2)

# Use apply() to calculate the mean of each column
col_means <- apply(m, 2, mean)

# Print the column means
print(col_means)
```

In this example, we create a matrix m with two columns and three rows. We then use the apply() function to calculate the mean of each column in the matrix by specifying margin = 2. The resulting col_means vector contains the mean of each column.

The apply() function is very flexible and can be used with any function that takes a vector or matrix as input. For example, we could use apply() to apply a custom function to each row of a data frame:

```
# Create a data frame
df <- data.frame(x = c(1, 2, 3), y = c(4, 5, 6))

# Define a custom function to apply to each row
row_product <- function(row) {
    return(prod(row))
}

# Use apply() to apply the function to each row
row_products <- apply(df, 1, row_product)

# Print the row products
print(row_products)
```

In this example, we create a data frame df with two columns and three rows. We then define a custom function row_product that takes a row of the data frame and returns the product of the row's values. We use apply() to apply this function to each row of the data frame by specifying margin = 1. The resulting row_products vector contains the product of each row.

In summary, the apply() function is a powerful and flexible tool for applying a function to a data set in R. It can be used with any type of R object that can be treated as a matrix or array, and can be used with any function that takes a vector or matrix as input.

3.5   What is the difference between deep and shallow copies of objects in R? How do you create each type of copy?

In R, copying an object creates a new object with the same values as the original object. However, there are two types of copies in R: deep copies and shallow copies.

A shallow copy (also called a "reference copy") creates a new object that points to the same memory location as the original object. This means that any changes made to the new object will also affect the original object. Shallow copies are created using the assignment operator ($<$-) or the $=$ operator.

Here's an example of creating a shallow copy in R:

```
# Create a vector
x <- c(1, 2, 3)

# Create a shallow copy of the vector
y <- x

# Change a value in the new vector
y[1] <- 10

# Print both vectors
print(x)
print(y)
```

In this example, we create a vector x with three elements, and then create a shallow copy of x called y. We then change the first element of y to 10, and print both x and y. Since y is a shallow copy of x, the change to y also affects x, and both vectors will contain the value 10 in the first position.

A deep copy creates a new object with the same values as the original object, but in a separate memory location. This means

that changes made to the new object will not affect the original
object. Deep copies can be created using functions such as
clone(), copy(), and dput().

Here's an example of creating a deep copy in R:

```
# Create a vector
x <- c(1, 2, 3)

# Create a deep copy of the vector
y <- clone(x)

# Change a value in the new vector
y[1] <- 10

# Print both vectors
print(x)
print(y)
```

In this example, we create a vector x with three elements, and
then create a deep copy of x called y using the clone() function.
We then change the first element of y to 10, and print both x
and y. Since y is a deep copy of x, the change to y does not
affect x, and the vectors will have different values.

In summary, the difference between deep and shallow copies
in R is that a shallow copy creates a new object that points
to the same memory location as the original object, while a
deep copy creates a new object in a separate memory location.
Shallow copies are created using the assignment operator or the
= operator, while deep copies are created using functions such
as clone(), copy(), and dput().

3.6 How do you handle and import data from Excel files in R?

Handling and importing data from Excel files in R is a common task for data analysts and scientists. There are several packages in R that can handle Excel files, including readxl, openxlsx, and xlsx.

Here's an example of how to use the readxl package to import data from an Excel file in R:

```
# Load the readxl package
library(readxl)

# Read data from an Excel file
my_data <- read_excel("my_file.xlsx", sheet = "Sheet1")

# Print the data
print(my_data)
```

In this example, we first load the readxl package. We then use the read_excel() function to read data from an Excel file called my_file.xlsx. We specify the name of the sheet to read using the sheet argument. The resulting my_data object is a data frame containing the data from the Excel sheet.

Another common package for handling Excel files in R is openxlsx. Here's an example of how to use openxlsx to write data to an Excel file:

```
# Load the openxlsx package
library(openxlsx)

# Create a data frame
my_data <- data.frame(x = c(1, 2, 3), y = c(4, 5, 6))

# Write the data to an Excel file
write.xlsx(my_data, "my_file.xlsx", sheetName = "Sheet1")
```

In this example, we first load the openxlsx package. We then create a data frame my_data. We use the write.xlsx() function to write the data to an Excel file called my_file.xlsx and specify the sheet name using the sheetName argument.

Both readxl and openxlsx are powerful packages for handling Excel files in R, and there are many other packages available as well. When working with Excel files in R, it's important to ensure that the data is in a suitable format for analysis (such as a tidy data format) and to handle any missing or inconsistent data appropriately.

3.7   Describe the split-apply-combine strategy in R and provide an example using the aggregate() function.

The split-apply-combine strategy is a common data analysis strategy used in R and other programming languages. The strategy involves splitting a data set into subsets based on one or more variables, applying a function to each subset, and then combining the results into a single data structure. This strategy is particularly useful when analyzing data with multiple groups or categories.

One function in R that can be used for split-apply-combine analysis is aggregate(). Here's an example of how to use aggregate() to calculate the mean of a variable by group:

```
# Create a data frame with two variables: group and value
df <- data.frame(group = rep(c("A", "B"), each = 4),
value = c(1, 2, 3, 4, 5, 6, 7, 8))

# Use aggregate() to calculate the mean of value by group
result <- aggregate(value ~ group, data = df, mean)
```

```
# Print the result
print(result)
```

In this example, we create a data frame df with two variables: group and value. We then use the aggregate() function to calculate the mean of value by group. The operator specifies that we want to group by group, and the data argument specifies the data frame to use. The mean function is applied to each subset of data, and the results are combined into a new data frame result. The resulting data frame result shows the mean value for each group.

The split-apply-combine strategy is a powerful tool for analyzing data in R, and the aggregate() function is just one example of a function that can be used for this purpose. Other functions that can be used for split-apply-combine analysis include tapply(), by(), and dplyr functions like group_by() and summarise().

3.8 Explain the concept of "vectorization" in R and why it is important.

In R, vectorization is the process of performing operations on entire vectors or arrays of data, rather than on individual elements. This allows for more efficient and concise code, as well as easier manipulation of large data sets.

For example, consider the following code that calculates the sum of two vectors using a loop:

```
# Create two vectors
a <- c(1, 2, 3)
```

```
b <- c(4, 5, 6)

# Calculate the sum of the two vectors using a loop
result <- numeric(length(a))
for (i in seq_along(a)) {
    result[i] <- a[i] + b[i]
}

# Print the result
print(result)
```

This code works, but it requires a loop to iterate over each element of the vectors and perform the addition operation. In contrast, here's an example of how the same calculation can be vectorized using the + operator:

```
# Create two vectors
a <- c(1, 2, 3)
b <- c(4, 5, 6)

# Calculate the sum of the two vectors using vectorization
result <- a + b

# Print the result
print(result)
```

This code produces the same result as the previous example, but it does so without the need for a loop. Instead, the + operator is applied element-wise to the entire vectors, resulting in a more concise and efficient implementation.

Vectorization is an important concept in R because it allows for more efficient and readable code, particularly when working with large data sets. Many functions in R are designed to work with vectors and arrays of data, and taking advantage of vectorization can result in significant performance improvements. Additionally, vectorized code is often easier to read and understand, making it more maintainable and less prone to errors.

3.9 What is the difference between rbind() and cbind() functions in R? Provide examples.

In R, rbind() and cbind() are both functions used for combining data frames or matrices, but they differ in how they combine the data.

rbind() stands for "row bind" and is used to combine data frames or matrices by adding rows. Here's an example:

```
# Create two data frames
df1 <- data.frame(x = c(1, 2, 3), y = c(4, 5, 6))
df2 <- data.frame(x = c(4, 5, 6), y = c(7, 8, 9))

# Use rbind() to combine the data frames
result <- rbind(df1, df2)

# Print the result
print(result)
```

In this example, we create two data frames df1 and df2 with two columns each. We use the rbind() function to combine the data frames by adding the rows of df2 below the rows of df1. The resulting data frame result has six rows and two columns.

cbind() stands for "column bind" and is used to combine data frames or matrices by adding columns. Here's an example:

```
# Create two data frames
df1 <- data.frame(x = c(1, 2, 3), y = c(4, 5, 6))
df2 <- data.frame(z = c(7, 8, 9))

# Use cbind() to combine the data frames
result <- cbind(df1, df2)

# Print the result
print(result)
```

In this example, we create two data frames df1 and df2. df1 has two columns, while df2 has one column. We use the cbind() function to combine the data frames by adding the column of df2 to the right of df1. The resulting data frame result has three columns and three rows.

In summary, rbind() combines data frames or matrices by adding rows, while cbind() combines data frames or matrices by adding columns. The choice between the two functions depends on the desired outcome and the structure of the data being combined.

3.10   How do you create a custom R function? Explain the structure and syntax.

Creating custom functions is an essential skill for R programmers. A custom function is a block of code that performs a specific task and can be called by the user multiple times. Here's how to create a custom function in R:

```
# Define a custom function
my_function <- function(arg1, arg2) {
    # Code block to perform the desired task
    result <- arg1 + arg2
    return(result)
}

# Call the custom function
my_result <- my_function(2, 3)

# Print the result
print(my_result)
```

In this example, we define a custom function called my_function using the function() keyword. The function takes two arguments, arg1 and arg2, and performs the task of adding them together. The result of the addition is stored in a variable called result, and the function returns this variable using the return() keyword.

To call the custom function, we simply use the function name followed by the arguments we want to pass in. In this case, we pass in the arguments 2 and 3, which results in a return value of 5. The resulting value is stored in the variable my_result, which we then print to the console.

The basic structure of a custom function in R consists of the following elements:

- The function() keyword, which is used to define the function

- A set of parentheses containing the function's arguments (if any)

- A code block containing the instructions to be executed when the function is called

- A return() statement (optional) that specifies the value that the function should return

When defining a custom function, it's important to choose a descriptive name that accurately reflects the task the function performs. Additionally, it's helpful to add comments or documentation to the function to describe its purpose, input arguments, and return values.

Overall, custom functions are an essential tool for R programmers and can be used to improve code readability, modularity, and reusability.

3.11   What is a package namespace in R? Why is it important?

In R, a package namespace is a mechanism that allows package developers to control the visibility of objects and functions within their package. A namespace acts as a "container" for the package's code and data, and determines how that code and data can be accessed by other packages or by users of the package.

The main purpose of a namespace is to prevent conflicts between objects and functions in different packages. Without a namespace, objects and functions with the same name could collide, causing unexpected behavior or errors. By using a namespace, package developers can ensure that their objects and functions are only accessible within the package, unless they are explicitly exported.

Here's an example of how a namespace works in R:

Suppose we have a package called mypackage that contains a function called myfunction(). Without a namespace, this function would be accessible to any other package or user of R by simply calling myfunction(). However, by using a namespace, we can control the visibility of myfunction() and other objects within the package.

To create a namespace for mypackage, we would create a file called NAMESPACE in the package's directory. This file contains a set of directives that specify which objects and functions should be exported (made visible) outside the package, and which should be kept private.

For example, the following code in the NAMESPACE file would export the myfunction() function:

```
# Export the myfunction() function
export(myfunction)
```

This means that other packages or users of R can access myfunction() by calling mypackage::myfunction(). However, any other objects or functions within the mypackage package would be hidden from view, unless they are explicitly exported in the NAMESPACE file.

In summary, package namespaces are an important feature of R packages because they allow developers to control the visibility of their code and prevent conflicts with other packages. By using namespaces, package developers can ensure that their code is modular, maintainable, and easy to use.

3.12   What are anonymous functions in R and how do you create one?

In R, an anonymous function is a function without a name. It's a short, one-line function that is defined on the fly and used immediately without assigning it to a variable. Anonymous functions are also known as "lambda functions" or "function literals."

Here's an example of how to create an anonymous function in R using the function() keyword:

```
# Define an anonymous function to square a number
squared <- function(x) x^2

# Use the anonymous function to square the number 3
result <- squared(3)
```

```
# Print the result
print(result)
```

In this example, we define an anonymous function using the function() keyword. The function takes one argument x and returns its square. We then call the function with the argument 3 and store the result in a variable called result, which we print to the console.

Anonymous functions are commonly used in R with functions like apply(), lapply(), and sapply(), where a short function needs to be passed as an argument. Here's an example using sapply() to calculate the squares of a vector of numbers:

```
# Create a vector of numbers
numbers <- c(1, 2, 3, 4, 5)

# Use sapply() and an anonymous function to square each
    number
squared <- sapply(numbers, function(x) x^2)

# Print the result
print(squared)
```

In this example, we use sapply() to apply an anonymous function to each element of the numbers vector. The anonymous function takes one argument x and returns its square. The resulting vector squared contains the squares of each number in numbers.

In summary, anonymous functions are a convenient way to define short, one-line functions on the fly in R. They are useful for passing functions as arguments to other functions or for creating simple, reusable functions without defining them as separate objects.

3.13 Explain the concept of "lazy evaluation" in R and provide an example.

In R, lazy evaluation is a concept where expressions are not evaluated until they are needed. This means that R will only compute the value of an expression when it is actually required, rather than computing it upfront.

Lazy evaluation is important in R because it can help to optimize code performance and memory usage. It allows R to delay expensive computations until they are actually needed, and can also help to avoid unnecessary computations altogether.

Here's an example of lazy evaluation in R:

```
# Define a function that takes two arguments
my_function <- function(x, y) {
   # Check if x is greater than 0
   if (x > 0) {
      # If x is greater than 0, return x * y
      return(x * y)
   } else {
      # If x is less than or equal to 0, return y
      return(y)
   }
}

# Call the function with x = 2 and y = 5
result <- my_function(2, 5)

# Print the result
print(result)
```

In this example, we define a function called my_function() that takes two arguments, x and y. The function checks if x is greater than 0. If it is, it returns the product of x and y. If it's not, it simply returns y.

The key point here is that the expression x * y is only evaluated if x > 0. If x is less than or equal to 0, then the expression is never evaluated. This is an example of lazy evaluation because R only computes the value of x * y when it is actually needed, rather than computing it upfront.

Lazy evaluation is a powerful concept in R because it allows for more efficient use of memory and computation resources. By delaying the evaluation of expressions until they are actually needed, R can optimize performance and improve the speed of complex computations.

3.14   What is the difference between seq() and rep() functions in R? Provide examples.

In R, seq() and rep() are two functions that are used to create sequences of values. However, they have different functionalities and are used in different contexts.

The seq() function is used to create sequences of evenly spaced values. It takes three arguments: from, to, and by, which specify the starting value, the ending value, and the increment between values. Here's an example:

```
# Create a sequence of values from 1 to 10, incrementing by
    2
my_seq <- seq(from = 1, to = 10, by = 2)

# Print the sequence
print(my_seq)
```

In this example, we use the seq() function to create a sequence of values from 1 to 10, incrementing by 2. The resulting sequence is 1 3 5 7 9.

On the other hand, the rep() function is used to repeat values. It takes two arguments: x, which specifies the values to repeat, and times, which specifies the number of times to repeat those values. Here's an example:

```
# Repeat the values "a" and "b" three times each
my_rep <- rep(c("a", "b"), times = 3)

# Print the repetition
print(my_rep)
```

In this example, we use the rep() function to repeat the values "a" and "b" three times each. The resulting repetition is "a" "b" "a" "b" "a" "b".

In summary, the seq() function is used to create sequences of evenly spaced values, while the rep() function is used to repeat values. While both functions can create sequences of values, they are used in different contexts and have different functionalities.

3.15   How do you use regular expressions in R for pattern matching and text manipulation?

In R, regular expressions are used for pattern matching and text manipulation. Regular expressions are a sequence of characters that define a search pattern. They are used to match and manipulate text based on a set of rules and patterns.

R has built-in support for regular expressions through the grep()

and gsub() functions, which are used to search for and replace text based on regular expressions.

Here's an example of using regular expressions in R to search for a pattern in a string:

```
# Define a string to search for a pattern
my_string <- "The quick brown fox jumps over the lazy dog."

# Use grep() to search for the pattern "fox"
found <- grep("fox", my_string)

# Print the result
print(found)
```

In this example, we use the grep() function to search for the pattern "fox" in the my_string variable. The function returns the index of the matching string, which in this case is 5.

Regular expressions can also be used for text manipulation, such as replacing text or extracting substrings. Here's an example of using regular expressions in R to replace text:

```
# Define a string to replace text
my_string <- "The quick brown fox jumps over the lazy dog."

# Use gsub() to replace the word "fox" with "cat"
new_string <- gsub("fox", "cat", my_string)

# Print the result
print(new_string)
```

In this example, we use the gsub() function to replace the word "fox" with "cat" in the my_string variable. The function returns a new string with the replacement made.

R provides a range of regular expression operators and functions that can be used for more complex pattern matching and text manipulation. Some of the commonly used operators include for the start of a string, $ for the end of a string, . for any character, [] for character classes, and | for alternation.

In summary, regular expressions are a powerful tool in R for pattern matching and text manipulation. By using a set of rules and patterns, regular expressions can be used to search for and replace text in a flexible and efficient way.

3.16 Describe the concepts of "scope" and "environments" in R and how they impact variable visibility.

In R, "scope" refers to the set of variables that are visible and accessible within a particular part of a program. The scope of a variable is determined by where it is defined and can be influenced by the use of functions and control structures.

"Environments" are a key concept in R that are closely related to scope. Environments are objects in R that contain a set of bindings between names and values. In other words, an environment is a collection of variables and functions that are defined within a particular scope.

In R, variables that are defined outside of a function have a global scope, meaning they are visible and accessible throughout the entire program. Variables that are defined within a function have a local scope, meaning they are only visible and accessible within that function.

Here's an example of how scope and environments work in R:

```
# Define a variable with global scope
my_var <- 10
```

```
# Define a function that uses a local variable
my_function <- function() {
    # Define a variable with local scope
    my_var <- 5

    # Print the local variable
    print(my_var)

    # Print the global variable
    print(get("my_var", envir = parent.frame()))
}

# Call the function
my_function()
```

In this example, we define a variable called my_var with global scope, meaning it is visible and accessible throughout the entire program. We also define a function called my_function that defines a variable with local scope called my_var.

When we call my_function(), it prints the value of my_var within the function, which is 5. It then prints the value of my_var in the global environment by using the get() function and specifying the parent frame as the environment to search for the variable. In this case, the parent frame is the global environment, so it prints the value of my_var as 10.

In summary, scope and environments are important concepts in R that determine the visibility and accessibility of variables within a program. By understanding how scope and environments work, you can write more efficient and effective R code.

3.17   What is the purpose of the str() function in R and how is it useful for data exploration?

In R, the str() function is used to display the structure of an R object. It provides information about the type and class of the object, the number of elements it contains, and the structure of its elements. The str() function is particularly useful for data exploration because it allows you to quickly and easily understand the structure of your data.

Here's an example of how the str() function can be used:

```
# Create a data frame
my_df <- data.frame(
name = c("Alice", "Bob", "Charlie"),
age = c(25, 30, 35),
married = c(TRUE, FALSE, TRUE)
)

# Use str() to display the structure of the data frame
str(my_df)
```

In this example, we create a data frame called my_df with three columns: name, age, and married. We then use the str() function to display the structure of the data frame.

The output of the str() function for this data frame would be:

```
'data.frame':   3 obs. of  3 variables:
$ name   : Factor w/ 3 levels "Alice","Bob","Charlie": 1 2
    3
$ age    : num  25 30 35
$ married: logi  TRUE FALSE TRUE
```

This output tells us that my_df is a data frame with 3 observations and 3 variables. It also tells us the class and type of each

variable: name is a factor with three levels, age is a numeric
variable, and married is a logical variable.

By using the str() function to explore the structure of our data,
we can gain insights into the types of variables we are working with and the format of the data. This can help us make
informed decisions about how to manipulate and analyze the
data.

In summary, the str() function is a powerful tool in R for data
exploration. By providing information about the structure and
type of an object, the str() function allows us to quickly and
easily understand the format of our data and make informed
decisions about how to work with it.

3.18   How do you visualize data in R us-
ing base graphics and ggplot2?

In R, there are two popular ways to visualize data: base graphics and ggplot2.

Base Graphics Base graphics are the built-in graphics system
in R. They provide a set of functions for creating plots, such as
plot(), hist(), and boxplot(). These functions are very flexible
and can be used to create a wide range of plot types.

Here's an example of how to create a scatter plot using base
graphics:

```
# Create a vector of x values
x <- c(1, 2, 3, 4, 5)

# Create a vector of y values
y <- c(2, 4, 3, 5, 1)
```

```
# Create a scatter plot
plot(x, y, main = "Scatter␣Plot", xlab = "X", ylab = "Y")
```

In this example, we create two vectors of data (x and y) and
then use the plot() function to create a scatter plot of the data.
We also add a title to the plot using the main argument and
label the x- and y-axes using the xlab and ylab arguments,
respectively.

ggplot2 ggplot2 is a popular package for creating graphics in R.
It provides a flexible and powerful system for creating a wide
range of visualizations using a consistent grammar of graphics.
The basic building blocks of ggplot2 plots are data, aesthetics
(the visual properties of the plot, such as color and size), and
geoms (the geometric shapes used to represent the data, such
as points, lines, and bars).

Here's an example of how to create a scatter plot using ggplot2:

```
# Load the ggplot2 package
library(ggplot2)

# Create a data frame
my_df <- data.frame(
    x = c(1, 2, 3, 4, 5),
    y = c(2, 4, 3, 5, 1)
)

# Create a scatter plot
ggplot(my_df, aes(x = x, y = y)) +
    geom_point() +
    labs(title = "Scatter␣Plot", x = "X", y = "Y")
```

In this example, we create a data frame called my_df with two
columns (x and y). We then use the ggplot() function to create
a ggplot object and specify the data and aesthetics of the plot
using the aes() function. We add points to the plot using the
geom_point() function and add a title and axis labels using the

labs() function.

Overall, both base graphics and ggplot2 provide powerful tools
for visualizing data in R. Base graphics are built-in and flexible, while ggplot2 provides a more structured and consistent
approach to creating graphics. Which system to use depends on
personal preference and the specific needs of the visualization.

3.19 Explain the concept of "recycling" in R and provide an example.

In R, "recycling" refers to the automatic replication of shorter
vectors to match the length of longer vectors during operations.
This feature is a powerful and convenient aspect of R that allows
you to apply a function to vectors of different lengths without
having to manually extend them.

Here's an example to illustrate the concept of recycling:

```
# Create two vectors
x <- c(1, 2, 3)
y <- c(4, 5)

# Add the vectors together
z <- x + y

# View the result
z
```

In this example, we create two vectors (x and y) with different
lengths. We then add the vectors together using the + operator.
Since x is longer than y, R automatically recycles y to match
the length of x before performing the operation. The resulting
vector z is the sum of each corresponding element of x and y,

with the shorter vector (y) repeated to match the length of the longer vector (x).

The resulting vector z would be:

```
[1] 5 7 7
```

This is because x[1] + y[1] is equal to 5, x[2] + y[2] is equal to 7, and x[3] + y[1] is equal to 7.

Recycling can also occur when using other operations, such as multiplication or division. For example:

```
# Create a vector
x <- c(1, 2, 3)

# Multiply the vector by a scalar
y <- x * 2

# View the result
y
```

In this example, we create a vector x and then multiply it by the scalar value 2. Since the length of the scalar value is 1, R automatically recycles it to match the length of x before performing the multiplication operation. The resulting vector y is the product of each element of x and the scalar value 2.

The resulting vector y would be:

```
[1] 2 4 6
```

Overall, the concept of recycling is a powerful and convenient feature of R that allows you to perform operations on vectors of different lengths without having to manually extend them.

3.20 How do you handle date and time objects in R? Provide examples using the lubridate package.

Handling date and time objects is a common task in data analysis and visualization, and R provides several packages to help with this task. One popular package for working with dates and times in R is lubridate.

Here's an overview of how to work with date and time objects in R using lubridate.

Creating Date and Time Objects

The lubridate package provides several functions for creating date and time objects in R. For example, you can create a date object using the ymd() function, which takes a character string in the format "year-month-day":

```
# Load the lubridate package
library(lubridate)

# Create a date object
my_date <- ymd("20220131")

# Print the date object
my_date
```

In this example, we create a date object called my_date using the ymd() function, which takes a character string representing a date in the format "year-month-day". The resulting object is a date object in R's default date format.

You can also create a time object using the hms() function, which takes a character string in the format "hours:minutes:seconds":

```
# Create a time object
my_time <- hms("12:30:15")

# Print the time object
my_time
```

In this example, we create a time object called my_time using the hms() function, which takes a character string representing a time in the format "hours:minutes:seconds". The resulting object is a time object in R's default time format.

Manipulating Date and Time Objects

Once you have created a date or time object in R, you can manipulate it using lubridate functions. For example, you can extract the year, month, or day from a date object using the year(), month(), or day() functions:

```
# Extract the year from the date object
my_year <- year(my_date)

# Extract the month from the date object
my_month <- month(my_date)

# Extract the day from the date object
my_day <- day(my_date)

# Print the results
my_year
my_month
my_day
```

In this example, we extract the year, month, and day from the date object my_date using the year(), month(), and day() functions, respectively.

You can also add or subtract time intervals from a date or time object using the add() or subtract() functions:

```
# Add 1 day to the date object
```

```
my_date_plus <- my_date %>% add(days = 1)

# Subtract 1 hour from the time object
my_time_minus <- my_time %>% subtract(hours = 1)

# Print the results
my_date_plus
my_time_minus
```

In this example, we add 1 day to the date object my_date
using the add() function and subtract 1 hour from the time
object my_time using the subtract() function.

Working with Time Zones

The lubridate package also provides functions for working with
time zones, such as with_tz() and force_tz(). For example, you
can convert a date or time object to a specific time zone using
the with_tz() function:

```
# Convert the date object to the "America/New_York" time
    zone
my_date_ny <- with_tz(my_date, "America/New_York")

# Print the result
my_date_ny
```

Chapter 4

Advanced

4.1 How do you optimize R code for performance? Provide examples of profiling tools and techniques.

Optimizing R code for performance is an important task when working with large datasets or complex computations. Here are some tips and techniques for improving R code performance:

1. Use vectorization: Vectorization is a technique for performing operations on entire vectors or arrays of data instead of looping over individual elements. This can greatly improve code performance in R. For example, instead of using a loop to calculate the sum of a vector, you can use the sum() function to perform the operation on the entire vector at once:

```
# Create a vector of values
my_vec <- c(1, 2, 3, 4, 5)
```

```
# Calculate the sum using a loop
my_sum <- 0
for (i in 1:length(my_vec)) {
    my_sum <- my_sum + my_vec[i]
}
my_sum

# Calculate the sum using the sum() function
my_sum2 <- sum(my_vec)
my_sum2
```

In this example, we compare two methods of calculating the sum of a vector. The first method uses a loop to iterate over the individual elements of the vector, while the second method uses the sum() function to perform the operation on the entire vector at once. The second method is faster and more efficient.

2. Use efficient data structures: Choosing the right data structure for your data can have a big impact on performance. For example, using a matrix instead of a data frame can be more efficient for certain operations, since matrices are stored as contiguous blocks of memory. Similarly, using a hash table instead of a list can improve performance for certain types of lookups.

3. Avoid unnecessary copies: Creating unnecessary copies of data can be a major performance bottleneck in R. To avoid this, use functions like subset() or filter() to subset data instead of creating a new copy of the entire dataset.

4. Use profiling tools: Profiling tools can help identify performance bottlenecks in your code. The profvis package provides a visual profiler for R code, which can help identify which parts of your code are taking the most time to execute:

```
# Install the profvis package
install.packages("profvis")

# Load the profvis package
library(profvis)
```

```
# Define a function to profile
my_func <- function(x) {
    y <- x^2 + sin(x)
    z <- sum(y)
    return(z)
}

# Profile the function
profvis(my_func(1:10000))
```

In this example, we use the profvis package to profile a simple function that performs some calculations on a vector. The resulting visualization shows which parts of the code are taking the most time to execute, allowing you to identify performance bottlenecks.

5. Use parallel processing: R supports parallel processing, which can be used to speed up certain types of computations. The parallel package provides tools for performing parallel computations in R:

```
# Load the parallel package
library(parallel)

# Define a function to perform a computation
my_func <- function(x) {
    y <- x^2 + sin(x)
    z <- sum(y)
    return(z)
}

# Generate some data
my_data <- list(1:10000, 10001:20000, 20001:30000)

# Use parallel processing to apply the function to each
    subset of data
my_results <- mclapply(my_data, my_func, mc.cores = 2)

# Combine the results
final_result <- sum(unlist(my_results))
```

In this example, we use the mclapply() function from the parallel package to apply a function to three subsets of data in parallel, using two cores.

4.2   What is the concept of "parallel computing" in R? Explain how to use the parallel package for parallel processing.

Parallel computing is a technique for performing computations using multiple processors or cores at the same time, which can greatly improve performance and reduce computation time. R supports parallel computing through the parallel package, which provides tools for executing code in parallel.

To use the parallel package, you need to first load the package using the library() function:

```
library(parallel)
```

The parallel package provides several functions for executing code in parallel, including:

- mclapply(): a parallel version of the lapply() function, which applies a function to a list in parallel.

- mcapply(): a parallel version of the apply() function, which applies a function to a matrix or array in parallel.

- clusterApply(): applies a function to a list or array on a cluster of machines.

- parLapply(): a parallel version of the lapply() function, which uses a cluster of machines.

- parSapply(): a parallel version of the sapply() function, which uses a cluster of machines.

Here's an example of how to use mclapply() to perform a computation in parallel:

```
# Define a function to be executed in parallel
my_func <- function(x) {
    # Perform some computation on x
    y <- x^2 + sin(x)
    z <- sum(y)
    return(z)
}

# Generate some data to work on
my_data <- list(1:10000, 10001:20000, 20001:30000)

# Apply the function to the data in parallel using mclapply
results <- mclapply(my_data, my_func, mc.cores = 2)

# Combine the results
final_result <- sum(unlist(results))
```

In this example, we define a function my_func that performs a computation on a vector of data. We then generate some data to work on and apply the function to the data in parallel using mclapply(). The mc.cores argument specifies the number of cores to use for the computation. Finally, we combine the results and obtain the final result.

Parallel computing can be a powerful tool for speeding up computations in R, especially when working with large datasets or complex computations. However, it's important to be aware of potential issues such as communication overhead and load balancing. It's also important to carefully test and benchmark code to ensure that it is actually faster when executed in parallel.

4.3   Explain the difference between S3 and S4 object systems in R. Provide examples of their usage.

In R, there are two object-oriented programming systems: S3 and S4. The S3 object system is the simpler of the two and is based on the idea of object-oriented programming as a way of organizing code. S4, on the other hand, is a more formal and structured system that provides more control and flexibility over object creation and manipulation.

S3 objects are created using the class() function, and methods are defined using the generic.function() syntax. Here is an example of creating an S3 object:

```
# Create an S3 object
my_obj <- list(data = 1:10, type = "numeric")
class(my_obj) <- "my_class"

# Define a method for my_class
my_method <- function(x, ...) {
   # Some code here
}

generic.function("my_method")
```

In this example, we create an S3 object my_obj using a list with two elements: data and type. We then assign the class "my_class" to the object using the class() function. Finally, we define a method for the my_class object using the generic.function() syntax.

S4 objects, on the other hand, are created using the setClass()
function and are defined with a formal structure that includes
slots, methods, and generics. Here is an example of creating an
S4 object:

```
# Create an S4 object
setClass("my_class", slots = list(data = "numeric", type =
    "character"))

# Define a method for my_class
setGeneric("my_method", function(object, ...)
    standardGeneric("my_method"))

setMethod("my_method", "my_class", function(object, ...) {
    # Some code here
})
```

In this example, we create an S4 object my_class using the
setClass() function, which defines two slots: data and type. We
then define a method for my_class using the setGeneric() and
setMethod() functions.

Overall, the main difference between S3 and S4 object systems
is their structure and formality. S4 objects are more formal and
structured, while S3 objects are more flexible and lightweight.
S3 is often used for simpler tasks, while S4 is preferred for more
complex and structured tasks.

4.4   Describe the concept of "functional programming" in R and its advantages. Provide examples using the purrr package.

Functional programming is a programming paradigm that emphasizes the use of functions to create reusable, composable, and modular code. In R, functional programming can be implemented using various packages, including the purrr package.

The purrr package provides a set of tools for functional programming in R, including functions for working with lists, vectors, and other data structures. Some of the key advantages of functional programming in R include:

Modularity: Functional programming encourages the use of small, modular functions that can be combined to create more complex operations. This can make code easier to read, understand, and maintain.

Reusability: Functions in functional programming are designed to be reusable, meaning they can be used in multiple contexts and applications.

Immutability: Functional programming emphasizes immutability, meaning that once a value is assigned to a variable, it cannot be changed. This can help to avoid bugs and ensure more predictable and stable code.

Here is an example of using the map() function from the purrr package to apply a function to each element of a list:

```
library(purrr)
```

```
# Create a list of numbers
my_list <- list(1, 2, 3, 4, 5)

# Define a function to multiply a number by 2
multiply_by_2 <- function(x) {
    x * 2
}

# Use map() to apply the function to each element of the
    list
result <- map(my_list, multiply_by_2)

# View the result
print(result)
```

In this example, we create a list of numbers called my_list. We then define a function called multiply_by_2 that multiplies a number by 2. Finally, we use the map() function from the purrr package to apply the function to each element of the list. The result is a new list where each element has been multiplied by 2.

Other functions in the purrr package, such as reduce(), filter(), and walk(), provide additional tools for functional programming in R. These functions can help to simplify code, improve performance, and make code more modular and reusable.

4.5   How do you create interactive web applications using R? Explain the role of the Shiny package.

R provides various packages for creating interactive web applications, but one of the most popular is the shiny package. The shiny package provides a set of tools for building web applications using R, without requiring any knowledge of HTML, CSS, or JavaScript.

The basic structure of a shiny application consists of two components: a user interface (UI) and a server. The UI component is responsible for defining the layout and appearance of the application, while the server component defines the behavior and functionality of the application.

Here's an example of a simple shiny application that allows the user to input a number and see its square:

```
library(shiny)

# Define UI
ui <- fluidPage(
numericInput("num", "Enter a number:", value = 0),
verbatimTextOutput("result")
)

# Define server
server <- function(input, output) {
    output$result <- renderText({
        paste("The square of", input$num, "is", input$num^2)
    })
}

# Run app
shinyApp(ui, server)
```

In this example, we first load the shiny package. We then define the UI component using the fluidPage() function. In this case, the UI consists of a numeric input field (numericInput()) and a text output field (verbatimTextOutput()).

Next, we define the server component using the server() function. This function takes two arguments: input, which contains the values of the input fields defined in the UI, and output, which defines the values to be displayed in the UI. In this example, the renderText() function is used to generate a text output based on the value entered in the input field.

Finally, we run the app using the shinyApp() function, which takes the UI and server components as arguments.

The shiny package provides a wide range of tools for building more complex web applications, including interactive plots, tables, and forms. It also provides various layout and formatting options, as well as support for custom CSS and JavaScript.

Overall, the shiny package makes it easy for R users to create interactive web applications, without needing to learn new programming languages or technologies.

4.6 Describe the use of the RMarkdown package for creating reproducible reports in R.

The RMarkdown package in R is a powerful tool for creating dynamic and reproducible reports, combining R code and text in a single document. With RMarkdown, you can easily create reports in a variety of formats, including HTML, PDF, and Word.

The basic idea behind RMarkdown is to create a document that mixes regular text with code chunks that can be executed by R. When the document is rendered, the code chunks are executed and the results are inserted into the final report.

Here's an example of a simple RMarkdown document:

```
---
title: "My First RMarkdown Document"
```

```
author: "John␣Doe"
date: "2022-03-30"
output: html_document
---

## Introduction
```

This is a simple example of an 'RMarkdown' document. We can include text, headers, and lists, just like in a regular document.

We can also include R code chunks, like this:

```
```{r}
x <- 1:10
mean(x)
```

The mean of x is r mean(x).

We can also include plots, like this:

```
plot(x, x^2, main = "Quadratic␣Function")
```

In this example, we first specify the document metadata, such as the title, author, and output format. We then write the main body of the document, which includes regular text and headers, as well as R code chunks enclosed in backticks ("').

When we render the document, the R code chunks are executed, and the results are inserted into the final report. In this case, we see the mean of 'x' and a plot of the quadratic function.

'RMarkdown' also allows you to include external files, such as data sets or images, and to use templates for consistent formatting across multiple documents. It also supports various output formats, including PDF, Word, and even presentations using the 'ioslides' or 'revealjs' frameworks.

Overall, the 'RMarkdown' package is a powerful tool for cre-
```

ating reproducible reports in R, allowing you to combine code, text, and visualizations in a single document.

4.7 Explain the concept of "memoization" in R and how it can be used to optimize function calls.

Memoization is a technique used in computer science to optimize the performance of functions that are called repeatedly with the same inputs. The idea is to cache the results of function calls so that if the same input is used again, the function can simply return the cached result instead of recomputing it.

In R, the memoise package provides a simple way to implement memoization for functions. To use memoization, we wrap our function with the memoise function, which returns a new function that automatically caches its results.

Here's an example of how to use the memoise package:

```
library(memoise)

# Define a slow function to compute Fibonacci numbers
fib <- function(n) {
   if (n <= 1) return(n)
   return(fib(n - 1) + fib(n - 2))
}

# Wrap the function with memoise
memo_fib <- memoise(fib)

# Compute the 10th Fibonacci number
memo_fib(10)  # returns 55

# Compute it again - this time it's faster!
   memo_fib(10)  # returns 55 (cached result)
```

In this example, we define a slow function fib that computes Fibonacci numbers recursively. We then wrap the function with memoise to create a new function memo_fib that automatically caches its results. When we call memo_fib(10) for the first time, it computes the result as usual. However, when we call it again with the same input, it returns the cached result instead of recomputing it.

Memoization can be especially useful for functions that are called frequently with the same inputs, or for functions that take a long time to compute. By caching the results, we can avoid redundant computation and speed up our code. However, memoization can also use a lot of memory if the function has many possible inputs, so it's important to use it judiciously and consider the memory requirements of our code.

4.8   How do you connect to and work with databases in R? Provide examples using the DBI package.

In R, we can connect to databases using the DBI package, which provides a consistent API for working with various database management systems.

To connect to a database, we need to first install the appropriate database driver package, such as RMySQL for MySQL databases or RSQLite for SQLite databases. Once the driver package is installed, we can use the dbConnect() function from the DBI package to establish a connection to the database.

Here's an example of how to connect to a MySQL database

using the RMySQL driver package and the DBI package:

```
library(DBI)
library(RMySQL)

# Connect to the database
con <- dbConnect(RMySQL::MySQL(),
dbname = "mydatabase",
host = "localhost",
port = 3306,
user = "myusername",
password = "mypassword")

# Query the database
result <- dbGetQuery(con, "SELECT * FROM mytable")

# Close the connection
dbDisconnect(con)
```

In this example, we first load the DBI and RMySQL packages. We then use the dbConnect() function to establish a connection to a MySQL database, specifying the database name, host, port, username, and password. We can then use the dbGetQuery() function to execute a SQL query on the database and retrieve the results. Finally, we use the dbDisconnect() function to close the connection to the database.

Once we have established a connection to the database, we can use the DBI functions to interact with the database, such as executing queries and retrieving results. The DBI package provides a consistent interface for working with different database systems, making it easy to switch between different databases without having to change our code.

4.9   What is the role of unit testing in R programming? Explain the use of the testthat package.

Unit testing is a software development practice that involves testing individual units or components of code to ensure they behave as expected. In R programming, unit testing can help us catch errors and bugs early in the development process, making it easier to maintain and improve our code over time.

The testthat package is a popular package in R for unit testing. It provides a simple framework for defining and running tests, as well as functions for comparing actual and expected results.

Here's an example of how to use the testthat package to test a simple function:

```
# Define a function to test
add <- function(x, y) {
    x + y
}

# Define a test using testthat
library(testthat)
test_that("add function works", {
    expect_equal(add(1, 2), 3)
    expect_equal(add(0, 0), 0)
})
```

In this example, we define a simple function called add() that adds two numbers together. We then use the test_that() function from testthat to define a test for the add() function. Within the test, we use the expect_equal() function to compare the actual result of calling add() with the expected result.

We can run our tests using the test_dir() function, which runs all tests in a specified directory:

```
test_dir("tests")
```

In this example, we assume that our test file is located in a directory called tests. When we run the test_dir() function, it will automatically run all tests in the tests directory and report any failures.

By using unit tests with a package like testthat, we can ensure that our code behaves as expected, even as it evolves over time. This can help us catch errors and bugs early in the development process, making it easier to maintain and improve our code.

4.10 Describe how to work with API endpoints in R using the httr package.

API (Application Programming Interface) endpoints provide a way for programs to interact with web services and access data or functionality provided by those services. In R, we can work with API endpoints using the httr package, which provides functions for making HTTP requests and handling the resulting data.

Here's an example of how to use the httr package to interact with a simple API:

```
library(httr)

# Define the endpoint URL
url <- "https://jsonplaceholder.typicode.com/todos/1"

# Make a GET request to the endpoint
response <- GET(url)
```

```
# Check the status code of the response
status_code(response)

# Extract the content of the response
content(response)

# Convert the response to a data frame
data <- fromJSON(content(response, "text"))
```

In this example, we first load the httr package. We then define the URL of an API endpoint that provides information about a specific task. We use the GET() function from httr to make a GET request to the endpoint, which returns a response object.

We can check the status code of the response using the status_code() function. In this case, we should see a status code of 200, which indicates that the request was successful.

We can extract the content of the response using the content() function. By default, this will return the content as a character string. We can then use the fromJSON() function from the jsonlite package to convert the content to a data frame.

From here, we can use standard R functions to manipulate and analyze the data as needed.

When working with APIs in R, it's important to understand the specific format and requirements of the API you're working with. Many APIs require authentication, for example, or may have specific endpoints and parameters that you need to use to access the data you're interested in. The httr package provides a flexible and powerful set of tools for working with APIs in R, but it's important to read the documentation and understand the specific requirements of the API you're working with.

4.11   How do you handle large datasets in R, both in memory and on disk? Provide examples using the data.table and ff packages.

Handling large datasets in R can be challenging, particularly if the data cannot be loaded into memory all at once. Fortunately, there are several packages in R that provide tools for working with large datasets both in memory and on disk. Two popular packages for this purpose are data.table and ff.

data.table is a package that provides an efficient and fast way to work with large datasets in memory. Here's an example of how to use data.table to work with a large dataset:

```
library(data.table)

# Generate a large dataset with 1 million rows and 3
    columns
dt <- data.table(x = rnorm(1000000), y = rnorm(1000000), z
    = rnorm(1000000))

# Subset the dataset using the i argument
dt[x > 0 & y < 0, .(mean(z), sum(z))]

# Aggregate the dataset using the by argument
dt[, .(mean(z), sum(z)), by = .(x > 0)]
```

In this example, we first load the data.table package. We then generate a large dataset with 1 million rows and 3 columns using the data.table() function. We can subset the dataset using the i argument, which works similarly to the square bracket notation for subsetting data frames. We can also aggregate the dataset using the by argument, which works similarly to the group_by() function in the dplyr package.

ff is a package that provides a way to work with large datasets
that cannot be loaded into memory all at once. Here's an example of how to use ff to work with a large dataset:

```
library(ff)

# Generate a large dataset with 1 million rows and 3
    columns
ffdf <- as.ffdf(data.frame(x = rnorm(1000000), y = rnorm
    (1000000), z = rnorm(1000000)))

# Subset the dataset using the [ and %subset% operators
ffdf[ffdf$x > 0 & ffdf$y < 0, cbind(mean(ffdf$z), sum(
    ffdf$z))]

# Aggregate the dataset using the ffbase package
library(ffbase)
ffdf_agg <- aggregate.ffdf(ffdf, by = list(x = ffdf$x > 0),
    FUN = list(mean = mean, sum = sum))
```

In this example, we first load the ff package. We then generate a large dataset with 1 million rows and 3 columns using
the as.ffdf() function. We can subset the dataset using the
square bracket notation, but for efficiency we can also use the
%subset% operator. We can aggregate the dataset using the
aggregate.ffdf() function from the ffbase package.

Both data.table and ff provide efficient and powerful tools for
working with large datasets in R. Which package is best for a
given task will depend on the specifics of the dataset and the
analysis being performed.

4.12 Explain the concept of "web scraping" in R and provide examples using the rvest package.

Web scraping is the process of extracting data from websites. R provides several packages for web scraping, including the popular rvest package. The rvest package provides functions for parsing and extracting data from HTML and XML files.

To use the rvest package, we first need to install it using the install.packages() function:

```
install.packages("rvest")
```

Once the package is installed, we can load it using the library() function:

```
library(rvest)
```

The main function in the rvest package is the read_html() function, which retrieves the HTML content of a webpage and stores it as an R object. We can then use other functions in the package to extract the data we need.

For example, let's say we want to extract the titles and URLs of the top news stories from the New York Times website. We can use the following code:

```
url <- "https://www.nytimes.com/"
page <- read_html(url)

# extract the titles
titles <- page %>% html_nodes(".story-heading") %>%
    html_text()

# extract the URLs
urls <- page %>% html_nodes(".story-heading a") %>%
    html_attr("href")
```

In this example, we first use the read_html() function to retrieve the HTML content of the New York Times homepage. We then use the %>% operator, which is part of the magrittr package, to pipe the page object into the html_nodes() function. This function selects all nodes that match a specified CSS selector. We use the .story-heading selector to select the nodes that contain the news story titles, and the .story-heading a selector to select the nodes that contain the story URLs.

We then use the html_text() function to extract the text content of the title nodes, and the html_attr() function to extract the "href" attribute of the URL nodes.

Finally, we can combine the titles and URLs into a data frame using the data.frame() function:

```
news <- data.frame(title = titles, url = urls)
```

This is just a simple example, but web scraping can be used for a wide range of tasks, such as monitoring competitors, gathering research data, and tracking social media activity. However, it's important to be aware of the legal and ethical implications of web scraping, as it can potentially violate website terms of service or privacy policies.

4.13   How do you create custom ggplot2 themes and geoms for data visualization in R?

The ggplot2 package in R provides a powerful system for creating complex and customizable visualizations of data. While the default themes and geoms provided by ggplot2 are often sufficient, it is sometimes useful to create custom themes and geoms to better represent the data being analyzed.

A ggplot2 theme is a set of formatting rules that can be applied to a plot to change its appearance. For example, a theme might specify the color scheme, font size, and axis labels for a plot. Themes can be created using the theme() function, and they can be modified by changing specific theme elements. Here is an example of a custom theme that changes the background color and font size of a plot:

```
library(ggplot2)

# create a custom theme
my_theme <- theme(
panel.background = element_rect(fill = "lightblue"),
text = element_text(size = 16)
)

# create a plot and apply the custom theme
ggplot(mtcars, aes(x = mpg, y = wt)) +
geom_point() +
labs(title = "My Plot") +
my_theme
```

A ggplot2 geom is a graphical object that can be added to a plot to represent data. For example, a geom might represent data points as circles, bars, or lines. Geoms can be created using the Geom*() functions, and they can be customized by modifying their parameters. Here is an example of a custom geom that represents data points as squares instead of circles:

```
library(ggplot2)

# create a custom geom
GeomSquare <- ggproto("GeomSquare", GeomPoint,
draw_panel = function(self, data, panel_params, coord) {
   data$shape <- 22
   GeomPoint$draw_panel(self, data, panel_params, coord)
}
)
```

```
# create a plot and apply the custom geom
ggplot(mtcars, aes(x = mpg, y = wt)) +
GeomSquare() +
labs(title = "My␣Plot")
```

In this example, we created a new GeomSquare object that inherits from the GeomPoint object, and we modified its draw_panel() method to change the shape of the data points to squares.

Overall, creating custom ggplot2 themes and geoms can be a powerful way to customize visualizations in R to better represent the data being analyzed.

4.14   Describe the use of the foreach package for parallel and sequential iterations in R.

The foreach package is a powerful tool for performing both parallel and sequential iterations in R. It provides a simple and flexible interface for defining loops that can be easily parallelized using different backends, such as doParallel, doMC, doMPI, and doSNOW.

The basic syntax of the foreach loop is as follows:

```
foreach(variable = iterable, . . . ) %dopar% {
    # loop body
}
```

where variable is the name of the loop variable, iterable is the sequence of values to loop over, and the %dopar% operator specifies that the loop should be executed in parallel.

Here is an example that demonstrates how to use the foreach

package to calculate the square of a list of numbers:

```
library(foreach)
library(doParallel)

# Create a list of numbers
nums <- list(1:5)

# Initialize the parallel backend
cl <- makeCluster(2)
registerDoParallel(cl)

# Define the foreach loop
result <- foreach(i = 1:length(nums), .combine = c) %dopar%
    {
    nums[[i]]^2
}

# Stop the parallel backend
stopCluster(cl)

# Print the result
print(result)
```

In this example, we first create a list of numbers called nums. We then initialize the parallel backend using the makeCluster function from the doParallel package, and register it with the registerDoParallel function.

Next, we define the foreach loop using the foreach function, where we iterate over the indices of the list nums and calculate the square of each element. We specify the .combine argument as c to combine the results into a single vector.

Finally, we stop the parallel backend using the stopCluster function and print the result.

The foreach package also provides a number of other features, such as the ability to handle nested loops, use of iterators, and support for error handling and progress bars.

4.15   What is the role of cross-validation in machine learning and how do you implement it in R?

Cross-validation is an essential technique used in machine learning to evaluate the performance of a model on unseen data. The main idea behind cross-validation is to split the available data into two sets: a training set and a validation set. The model is trained on the training set and evaluated on the validation set, which serves as a proxy for new, unseen data.

There are several types of cross-validation techniques available, but the most common ones are k-fold cross-validation and leave-one-out cross-validation.

K-fold cross-validation involves splitting the data into k equally-sized subsets or "folds". The model is trained on k-1 of these folds and evaluated on the remaining fold. This process is repeated k times, with each fold serving as the validation set exactly once. The final performance metric is the average of the performance metrics obtained on each of the k validation sets.

Here is an example of how to perform k-fold cross-validation using the caret package in R:

```
library(caret)
data(iris)

# define the control object for k-fold cross-validation
ctrl <- trainControl(method = "cv", number = 5)

# train the model using k-fold cross-validation
model <- train(Species ~ ., data = iris, method = "rf",
    trControl = ctrl)

# view the results
```

```
print(model)
```

In this example, we are using the random forest algorithm (specified by the "rf" method) to predict the species of iris flowers based on their sepal length, sepal width, petal length, and petal width. We are using a 5-fold cross-validation strategy (specified by the number = 5 argument), and the resulting model is stored in the model object.

Leave-one-out cross-validation (LOOCV) is a special case of k-fold cross-validation where k is equal to the number of observations in the dataset. In LOOCV, the model is trained on all observations except one, and the performance is evaluated on the remaining observation. This process is repeated for each observation in the dataset, and the final performance metric is the average of the performance metrics obtained on each iteration.

Here is an example of how to perform LOOCV using the caret package in R:

```
library(caret)
data(iris)

# define the control object for LOOCV
ctrl <- trainControl(method = "LOOCV")

# train the model using LOOCV
model <- train(Species ~ ., data = iris, method = "rf",
    trControl = ctrl)

# view the results
print(model)
```

In this example, we are using the random forest algorithm (specified by the "rf" method) to predict the species of iris flowers based on their sepal length, sepal width, petal length, and petal width. We are using LOOCV (specified by the method = "LOOCV" argument), and the resulting model is stored in the model object.

4.16   Explain the use of the caret package for creating and evaluating predictive models in R.

The caret package (short for Classification And REgression Training) is a popular package in R for creating and evaluating predictive models. It provides a streamlined workflow for building and evaluating models using a variety of machine learning algorithms, including linear regression, logistic regression, decision trees, random forests, and support vector machines.

The caret package offers several useful functions for data preprocessing, including missing value imputation, feature selection, and normalization. It also includes several tools for evaluating model performance, such as cross-validation, ROC curves, and confusion matrices.

To create a predictive model using the caret package, the following steps are typically followed:

Load the data: Use the appropriate R functions to load the data into a data frame or other suitable object.

Preprocess the data: Use functions from the caret package or other packages to impute missing values, normalize the data, and perform feature selection.

Split the data: Split the data into a training set and a test set using functions such as createDataPartition or sample.

Train the model: Use the train function to train the model using the training set and the desired machine learning algorithm.

Evaluate the model: Use the predict function to generate predictions on the test set, and then evaluate the model's performance using metrics such as accuracy, precision, recall, F1 score, and ROC curve.

Here is an example of using the caret package to create and evaluate a linear regression model:

```
library(caret)

# Load the data
data(mtcars)

# Split the data into a training set and a test set
set.seed(123)
trainIndex <- createDataPartition(mtcars$mpg, p = .8, list
    = FALSE)
trainData <- mtcars[trainIndex, ]
testData <- mtcars[-trainIndex, ]

# Train the model using linear regression
model <- train(mpg ~ ., data = trainData, method = "lm")

# Generate predictions on the test set and evaluate the
    model's performance
   predictions <- predict(model, newdata = testData)
   accuracy <- mean((predictions - testData$mpg)^2)
```

In this example, we first load the mtcars dataset and split it into a training set and a test set using the createDataPartition function. We then train the linear regression model using the train function and the training set. Finally, we use the predict function to generate predictions on the test set, and calculate the mean squared error as a measure of model performance.

The caret package provides many additional functions and options for fine-tuning the model creation and evaluation process.

It is a powerful and versatile tool for machine learning in R.

4.17   How do you perform text mining and natural language processing in R? Provide examples using the tm and tidytext packages.

Text mining and natural language processing (NLP) are common tasks in data science, which can be performed in R using various packages such as tm and tidytext. The tm package is specifically designed for text mining, whereas the tidytext package is part of the tidyverse ecosystem and focuses on tidy data principles.

The tm package provides tools for reading in text data, preprocessing, cleaning, and transforming text, and creating term-document matrices for modeling. For example, the following code reads in a corpus of text files and performs preprocessing steps such as removing stop words and stemming:

```
library(tm)
data("crude")
crude_corpus <- VCorpus(VectorSource(crude))
crude_corpus <- tm_map(crude_corpus, removeWords, stopwords
    ("english"))
crude_corpus <- tm_map(crude_corpus, stemDocument)
```

Once the text has been preprocessed, the next step is to create a term-document matrix (TDM) that represents the frequency of each term (word) in each document. This can be done using the DocumentTermMatrix() function:

```
crude_tdm <- DocumentTermMatrix(crude_corpus)
```

The resulting TDM can then be used for various types of analyses, such as clustering or topic modeling.

The tidytext package, on the other hand, provides tools for working with text data in a tidy format, which is more amenable to the tidyverse data manipulation tools. This includes functions for splitting text into words, creating n-grams, and performing sentiment analysis. For example, the following code reads in a data frame of customer reviews and calculates the frequency of each word using the unnest_tokens() function:

```
library(tidytext)
data("yelp")
yelp_words <- yelp %>%
unnest_tokens(word, text) %>%
count(word, sort = TRUE)
```

The resulting data frame can then be used for further analysis or visualization.

In addition to these packages, there are many other tools and techniques available in R for text mining and NLP, such as regular expressions, word embeddings, and deep learning models.

4.18   Describe the concept of "time series analysis" in R and provide examples using the xts and forecast packages.

Time series analysis is a statistical technique used to analyze and extract patterns from data that is indexed over time. In R, the xts (eXtensible Time Series) and forecast packages are widely used for time series analysis.

The xts package provides a specialized data structure called
an xts object, which extends the functionality of regular time
series objects in R. xts objects are used to store time series
data, with the time information stored in the index of the object. The package also provides functions for manipulating and
analyzing xts objects, such as time-based subsetting, merging,
aggregation, and rolling calculations.

Here's an example of using the xts package to create an xts
object from a data frame, and then calculating some summary
statistics:

```
library(xts)

# create a data frame with some time series data
df <- data.frame(
date = seq(as.Date("2022-01-01"), as.Date("2022-01-10"), by
    = "day"),
value = rnorm(10)
)

# convert the data frame to an xts object
xts_obj <- xts(df$value, order.by = df$date)

# calculate some summary statistics
mean_xts <- mean(xts_obj)
sd_xts <- sd(xts_obj)
```

The forecast package provides functions for time series forecasting and visualization. It includes a variety of models for
forecasting, such as exponential smoothing, ARIMA, and sea-
sonal decomposition of time series. The package also includes
functions for visualizing time series data and forecasting results.

Here's an example of using the forecast package to forecast
future values of a time series:

```
library(forecast)

# create a time series object with some random data
ts_obj <- ts(rnorm(100))
```

```
# forecast the next 10 values using an ARIMA model
forecast_obj <- forecast(auto.arima(ts_obj), h = 10)

# plot the original time series and the forecast
plot(forecast_obj)
```

Overall, the xts and forecast packages provide powerful tools for working with time series data in R, allowing for sophisticated analysis and forecasting.

4.19   What is the role of the devtools package in R package development? Explain its main features.

The devtools package is an R package that provides a set of tools for developing and maintaining other R packages. It includes functions for package installation, updating, testing, documentation, and more. The package makes it easier to develop packages in R and to share them with others.

Some of the main features of the devtools package include:

Package installation: The package provides functions for installing and updating packages from various sources, including GitHub, CRAN, and local files.

Example: Install the latest version of a package from CRAN using devtools

```
library(devtools)
install.packages("package_name")
```

Package development: The package includes functions for creating and managing package files, including functions for creating and updating the DESCRIPTION file, adding new functions to a package, and more.

Example: Create a new package with devtools

```
library(devtools)
create("package_name")
```

Package testing: The package includes functions for testing packages, including functions for running unit tests and generating code coverage reports.

Example: Run tests for a package using devtools

```
library(devtools)
test("package_name")
```

Package documentation: The package includes functions for generating documentation for packages, including functions for creating vignettes and generating help files.

Example: Create a vignette for a package using devtools

```
library(devtools)
use_vignette("my_vignette")
```

Package publishing: The package includes functions for publishing packages to CRAN and other repositories.

Example: Publish a package to CRAN using devtools

```
library(devtools)
check("package_name")
release("package_name")
```

Overall, the devtools package is a powerful tool for R package development and maintenance, and can save developers time and effort when working with packages in R.

4.20   How do you create and customize R package documentation using the roxygen2 package?

When creating an R package, documentation is an important aspect to ensure that the package is well-documented, easy to understand, and can be used by other developers. The roxygen2 package is a popular tool for creating documentation in R packages. It allows users to write documentation alongside the code itself using special syntax.

To use the roxygen2 package, we first need to install it using the following command:

```
install.packages("roxygen2")
```

Next, we need to use special syntax to write documentation alongside our R code. For example, to add a function documentation, we would write a comment block immediately preceding the function code, like this:

```
#' Function title
   #'
#' Function description goes here.
   #'
#' @param arg1 Description of arg1
   #' @param arg2 Description of arg2
#' @return Description of the output
   #' @examples
#' function_example()
   #' @export
   function_name <- function(arg1, arg2) {
      # function code goes here
   }
```

In the comment block, we use the #' notation to indicate that we are writing documentation. The first line is the title of the function, followed by a brief description of the function's purpose. We then use the @param notation to document each argument of the function, and the @return notation to describe the output of the function.

The @examples notation is used to provide examples of how to use the function. These examples will be run automatically when building the package to ensure that the function is working as expected.

Finally, we use the @export notation to indicate that the function should be exported from the package and made available to other packages and users.

Once we have written our documentation, we can use the roxygen2 package to automatically generate the package documentation files using the following command:

```
roxygen2::roxygenise()
```

This will create a man directory in our package directory, containing the HTML files with the function documentation.

In summary, the roxygen2 package is a powerful tool for creating documentation in R packages. It allows us to write documentation alongside our code using special syntax, and automatically generates the package documentation files.

Chapter 5

Expert

5.1 Explain the process of creating and submitting a package to CRAN, including the steps involved and requirements to meet.

Creating and submitting a package to the Comprehensive R Archive Network (CRAN) is a great way to share your code with the broader R community. However, the process can be challenging and time-consuming. Here is an overview of the steps involved and the requirements to meet:

Step 1: Develop the Package

The first step in creating a package is to write the code and documentation. The code should be written in R and should be well-documented, following the standards set by the roxygen2 package. The documentation should include the function and package descriptions, examples, and references.

Step 2: Prepare the Package for Submission

Once the package is developed, it needs to be prepared for submission to CRAN. This involves several steps, including:

- Creating a tarball of the package

- Checking the package for errors using the R CMD check command

- Creating a README file that includes instructions for installing and using the package

- Creating a NEWS file that includes a description of the changes made in each version of the package

- Creating a LICENSE file that specifies the terms under which the package can be used

Step 3: Submit the Package to CRAN

After the package is prepared, it can be submitted to CRAN. The submission process involves several steps:

- Create an account on the CRAN submission site

- Upload the tarball of the package

- Fill out the submission form, which includes information such as the package name, description, and author information

- Wait for the CRAN team to review the package

Step 4: Address Feedback from the CRAN Team

After the package is submitted, the CRAN team will review it and provide feedback. The feedback may include requests to fix errors, improve the documentation, or make other changes to the package. The package developer will need to address the feedback and resubmit the package for review.

Step 5: Package is Accepted

Once the package meets all the requirements and the CRAN team approves it, it will be included in the CRAN repository, and users can install it using the install.packages command.

In conclusion, creating and submitting a package to CRAN is a rigorous process, but it can be a rewarding way to share your code with the broader R community. By following the standards and guidelines, you can create a high-quality package that is easy to use and maintain.

5.2   How do you implement object-oriented programming in R using both S4 and R6 systems? Provide examples.

Object-oriented programming (OOP) is a programming paradigm that allows programmers to define data structures (called objects) that have attributes and behaviors. In R, there are two systems for implementing OOP: the S4 system and the R6 system.

S4 System

The S4 system is a formal, class-based system that provides explicit control over inheritance and dispatch. It is more complex than the S3 system but more powerful, allowing for more control over the behavior of objects. The following is an example of defining an S4 class in R:

```
setClass("Person",
    representation(
        name = "character",
        age = "numeric"
    )
)

person <- new("Person", name = "John", age = 30)
```

In this example, we define a new class called "Person" using the setClass() function. We define the class to have two attributes: name and age, which are of type character and numeric, respectively. We then create a new object of class Person called person using the new() function.

We can then define methods for our Person class using the setMethod() function. For example, we can define a method for printing out a summary of a Person object:

```
setMethod("summary", "Person",
function(object) {
    cat("Name:", object@name, "n")
    cat("Age:", object@age, "n")
}
)
```

summary(person)

In this example, we define a method for summary() that applies to objects of class Person. The method takes a single argument, object, which is an instance of the Person class. The method then prints out a summary of the object's name and age attributes using the cat() function.

R6 System

The R6 system is a simpler, reference-based system that is easier to learn and use. It provides a simpler syntax for defining classes and objects than the S4 system. The following is an example of defining an R6 class in R:

```
library(R6)

Person <- R6Class(
"Person",
public = list(
name = NULL,
age = NULL,
initialize = function(name, age) {
   self$name <- name
   self$age <- age
},
summary = function() {
   cat("Name:", self$name, "n")
   cat("Age:", self$age, "n")
}
)
)

person <- Person$new(name = "John", age = 30)
```

In this example, we define a new class called Person using the R6Class() function from the R6 package. We define the class to have two attributes: name and age. We also define an initialize() method that takes name and age arguments and sets the name and age attributes of the object. We also define a summary() method that prints out a summary of the object's name and age attributes using the cat() function.

We then create a new object of class Person called person using the $new() method.

In conclusion, both the S4 and R6 systems provide powerful tools for implementing OOP in R. The S4 system is more complex and provides more control over inheritance and dispatch, while the R6 system is simpler and easier to learn and use.

5.3 Describe best practices for managing dependencies and version control in R projects.

Managing dependencies and version control is an essential aspect of any R project. Here are some best practices for managing dependencies and version control in R projects:

Use a package manager: A package manager such as renv can help manage the dependencies of an R project. It creates a project-specific library of packages and ensures that packages used in the project are of the correct version.

Use version control: Use a version control system such as Git to keep track of changes made to the codebase. This helps to collaborate with other team members and ensure that the code is always in a stable state.

Use semantic versioning: Semantic versioning ensures that version numbers reflect the nature of the changes made to a package. The version number is structured as MAJOR.MINOR.PATCH, where MAJOR denotes a major change, MINOR denotes a minor change, and PATCH denotes a bug fix.

Document dependencies: Document the dependencies of an R project in a README file. This includes listing the packages used, their versions, and their purpose in the project.

Regularly update packages: Regularly update packages used in the project to ensure that they are up-to-date with the latest bug fixes and security patches.

Use continuous integration: Continuous integration ensures that the codebase is always in a stable state by running automated tests on every commit. This can be achieved using services such as Travis CI or Jenkins.

Use code reviews: Use code reviews to ensure that changes made to the codebase adhere to best practices, and to catch errors before they are merged into the main branch.

Use release branches: Use release branches to ensure that the code in production is always stable. Release branches are created from the main branch and contain only bug fixes and minor changes.

By following these best practices, you can ensure that your R projects are always in a stable state and can be easily maintained over time.

5.4   Explain the role of Continuous Integration (CI) and Continuous Deployment (CD) in R package development. Provide examples using tools such as GitHub Actions and Travis CI.

Continuous Integration (CI) and Continuous Deployment (CD) are important aspects of modern software development, including R package development. CI/CD is a software development practice that involves automating the testing and deployment of code changes. It enables developers to continuously integrate code changes into a shared repository and automatically test and deploy them, reducing the risk of bugs and errors in the code.

In R package development, CI/CD ensures that the package is continuously integrated, tested, and deployed to a specific environment (e.g., CRAN or a private repository) without any manual intervention. This ensures that the package is always up-to-date, stable, and functional.

GitHub Actions and Travis CI are two popular tools for implementing CI/CD in R package development. Both tools automate the process of building, testing, and deploying R packages.

GitHub Actions is a built-in feature of the GitHub platform that allows developers to create custom workflows for their projects. In R package development, a typical GitHub Actions workflow involves creating a series of jobs that perform tasks such as package installation, testing, and deployment. For example, a simple GitHub Actions workflow for an R package might include the following steps:

- Install dependencies

- Build package

- Run tests

- Deploy to CRAN

Here's an example of a simple GitHub Actions workflow for an R package:

```
name: R-CMD-check

on:
push:
branches: [main]

jobs:
R-CMD-check:
runs-on: macOS-latest

steps:
- uses: actions/checkout@v2
- name: Set up R
uses: r-lib/actions/setup-r@v1
with:
r-version: '4.1.0'
- name: Install dependencies
run: |
install.packages("devtools")
install.packages("testthat")
- name: Check package
run: |
devtools::check()
```

Travis CI is another popular CI/CD tool for R package development. It is a hosted service that automates the testing and deployment of code changes. A typical Travis CI workflow for an R package might include the following steps:

- Install dependencies

- Build package

- Run tests

- Deploy to CRAN

Here's an example of a simple Travis CI workflow for an R package:

```
language: r
cache: packages

before_install:
- R -e 'install.packages("devtools")'
- R -e 'devtools::install_deps()'

script:
- R CMD build .
- R CMD check *tar.gz --as-cran

deploy:
provider: script
script: Rscript -e 'devtools::release()'
skip_cleanup: true
on:
tags: true
```

In both examples, the workflow checks the R package by installing dependencies, building the package, running tests, and deploying it to a specific environment. This helps ensure that the package is always up-to-date, stable, and functional.

In addition to GitHub Actions and Travis CI, there are several other CI/CD tools that can be used for R package development, such as Jenkins, CircleCI, and GitLab CI/CD. Regardless of the tool used, the main goal of CI/CD in R package development is to automate the testing and deployment process, thereby reducing the risk of errors and increasing the speed and efficiency of the development process.

5.5 How do you manage large-scale R projects with multiple contributors? Discuss tools and practices for collaboration and organization.

Managing large-scale R projects with multiple contributors can be challenging, but there are several tools and practices that can help ensure a smooth collaboration and organization.

Version Control System: The first step in managing a large-scale project is to use a version control system (VCS) like Git. This allows all team members to work on the same codebase simultaneously and tracks all changes made to the code. GitHub is a popular hosting service that offers features like code review, issue tracking, and pull requests that can facilitate collaboration and organization.

Code Style Guide: It is important to establish a code style guide that all team members can follow. This includes guidelines on formatting, naming conventions, and commenting. The tidyverse style guide is a good starting point for establishing best practices.

Project Structure: It is important to have a clear project structure that makes it easy to find and organize files. The Project-Template package provides a framework for organizing data, code, and documentation in a consistent and reproducible way.

Documentation: Clear and concise documentation is critical for large-scale projects, especially if the project is being used by people outside the team. The roxygen2 package provides a convenient way to document code using inline comments.

Continuous Integration: Continuous Integration (CI) is a practice of automatically building and testing code changes as they
are made. This can help catch errors early and ensure that
the code is always in a working state. Travis CI and GitHub
Actions are popular CI tools that can be used for R projects.

Package Development: If the project involves creating an R
package, it is important to follow best practices for package
development. This includes creating unit tests, ensuring compatibility with different R versions and operating systems, and
submitting the package to CRAN or other repositories.

Communication: Effective communication is essential for successful collaboration. Regular meetings, email updates, and
chat tools like Slack can help keep everyone on the same page.

Example:

Suppose a team of data scientists is working on a large-scale
project to develop a machine learning model that predicts customer churn for a telecom company. The project involves multiple R scripts, datasets, and documentation files. Here are
some examples of how the team can implement best practices
for collaboration and organization:

- They use Git and GitHub to manage the codebase, track
  changes, and collaborate with each other.

- They establish a code style guide that includes guidelines
  on formatting, naming conventions, and commenting.

- They use ProjectTemplate to organize the data, code, and
  documentation files in a consistent and reproducible way.

- They use roxygen2 to document their code and ensure

that it is clear and concise.

- They set up Travis CI to automatically build and test code changes as they are made.

- They create an R package that includes the machine learning model and submit it to CRAN.

- They hold regular meetings and use Slack to communicate with each other and ensure that everyone is up to date on the project's progress.

By following these best practices, the team can work efficiently and effectively on the project, ensuring that the final product is of high quality and meets the requirements of the stakeholders.

5.6 Describe methods for handling and analyzing spatial data in R, including packages such as sf and sp.

R provides many powerful tools for working with spatial data, allowing users to import, visualize, and analyze data with geographic coordinates. In this answer, we will discuss some of the methods and packages commonly used for spatial data analysis in R.

The sf package is a popular package for handling spatial data in R. It provides classes and methods for working with vector data, including points, lines, and polygons. The package has a wide range of functions for importing, exporting, and transforming spatial data, as well as for working with projections and coordinate reference systems. The sf package also provides tools for visualizing spatial data, including ggplot2 integration.

Here is an example of how to use sf to plot the spatial distribution of earthquakes from the USGS database:

```
library(sf)
library(ggplot2)

# Import earthquake data
eq_data <- st_read("https://earthquake.usgs.gov/fdsnws/
    event/1/query?format=geojson&starttime=2020-01-01&
    endtime=2020-01-31")

# Plot the earthquake data
ggplot() +
geom_sf(data = eq_data, aes(fill = mag), size = 0.1) +
scale_fill_gradient(low = "yellow", high = "red") +
theme_void()
```

The sp package is another popular package for handling spatial data in R. It provides classes and methods for working with both vector and raster data, and has a wide range of functions for manipulating and analyzing spatial data. The sp package also provides support for working with projections and coordinate reference systems.

Here is an example of how to use sp to calculate the distance between points in two datasets:

```
library(sp)

# Create two sets of random points
set.seed(123)
points1 <- data.frame(x = rnorm(10), y = rnorm(10))
points2 <- data.frame(x = rnorm(10), y = rnorm(10))

# Convert the datasets to spatial points
coordinates(points1) <- ~x + y
coordinates(points2) <- ~x + y

# Calculate the distance between the points in each dataset
distances <- apply(gDistance(points1, points2), 1, min)
```

```
# Print the minimum distances
print(distances)
```

These are just a few examples of the many tools available for handling and analyzing spatial data in R. Depending on your specific needs, other packages such as leaflet and tmap may also be useful for visualizing spatial data or performing spatial analysis.

5.7 Explain advanced techniques for parallel and distributed computing in R, such as using the future and rhipe packages.

R provides several packages to perform parallel and distributed computing to speed up the computation of large datasets. Two of the popular packages for parallel computing in R are future and rhipe.

The future package provides a simple and consistent way to work with parallelism in R using a "future" abstraction. A "future" is an R expression that will be evaluated at some point in the future. The package provides a variety of backends, including local parallelism using multi-core CPUs, remote parallelism using SSH or MPI, and cloud computing using services such as Amazon EC2 or Microsoft Azure. Here is an example of how to use the future package to perform parallel computation:

```
library(future)
plan(multiprocess)

x <- 1:1000000
```

```
y <- future_lapply(x, sqrt)
```

In this example, we use plan(multiprocess) to set up a multi-core parallel processing backend. We then create a vector x and use future_lapply to apply the sqrt function to each element of x in parallel, returning a list of futures.

The rhipe package provides an interface between R and Hadoop, allowing users to process large datasets in parallel on a Hadoop cluster. The package provides functions for reading and writing data to Hadoop, as well as for performing distributed computations using MapReduce. Here is an example of how to use the rhipe package to perform a word count on a text file stored in Hadoop:

```
library(rhipe)

rhinit()
rhipe_input(file.path("hdfs:///path/to/input/file"))
rhipe_mapreduce(
input = "text",
output = "wordcount",
map = function(k, v) {
    words <- strsplit(v, "s")[[1]]
    rhcollect(list(zip(words, rep(1, length(words)))))
},
reduce = function(k, v) {
    rhcollect(list(k, sum(v)))
}
)
result <- rhread("wordcount")
```

In this example, we use rhinit() to initialize the rhipe package, and rhipe_input() to read in the text file stored in Hadoop. We then use rhipe_mapreduce() to perform a word count on the file, with the map function splitting the text into words and the reduce function summing up the counts for each word. Finally, we use rhread() to read the output of the MapReduce job into R.

Overall, the future and rhipe packages provide powerful tools for performing parallel and distributed computing in R, allowing users to take advantage of multi-core CPUs and Hadoop clusters to speed up computation on large datasets.

5.8 How do you develop custom algorithms for high-performance computing in R? Discuss using Rcpp for C++ integration.

R is a popular language for statistical computing and data analysis. It provides a rich set of libraries and tools for solving complex problems, and it has a large user community. However, for some computationally intensive tasks, R might not be the best choice. In such cases, Rcpp provides a seamless integration of C++ and R, allowing users to write high-performance algorithms with the benefits of both languages.

Rcpp is an R package that provides a C++ API for R, allowing R code to be embedded in C++ functions, and vice versa. The package provides a range of features, including automatic conversion between R and C++ data types, and seamless integration with Rs memory management system.

To develop custom algorithms for high-performance computing in R using Rcpp, you will need to follow these general steps:

- Write the algorithm in C++ using the Rcpp API

- Compile the C++ code into a shared library

- Load the shared library into R using the dyn.load() function

- Call the C++ functions from R

Here's an example of a simple C++ function that computes the sum of two vectors:

```
#include <Rcpp.h>
using namespace Rcpp;

// [[Rcpp::export]]
NumericVector add_vectors(NumericVector x, NumericVector y)
    {
    int n = x.size();
    NumericVector result(n);
    for (int i = 0; i < n; ++i) {
        result[i] = x[i] + y[i];
    }
    return result;
}
```

This function takes two NumericVector arguments and returns their element-wise sum. The [[Rcpp::export]] attribute is used to indicate that this function can be called from R.

Once you have written your C++ code, you can compile it into a shared library using the Rcpp package. Here's an example Makefile:

```
CXX_STD = CXX11
PKG_LIBS = $(shell $(R_HOME)/bin/Rscript -e "Rcpp:::LdFlags
    ()")

all: add_vectors.so

add_vectors.so: add_vectors.cpp
R CMD SHLIB -o $@ $< $(PKG_LIBS)
```

This Makefile specifies the C++11 standard and sets the PKG_LIBS variable to the flags needed to link against the Rcpp library. It then defines a target called add_vectors.so that depends on add_vectors.cpp. The R CMD SHLIB command is used to compile the shared library.

To load the shared library into R, you can use the dyn.load() function:

```
dyn.load("add_vectors.so")
```

Once the shared library is loaded, you can call the C++ function from R:

```
library(Rcpp)
x <- c(1, 2, 3)
y <- c(4, 5, 6)
add_vectors(x, y)
```

This will call the add_vectors() function defined in the C++ code, passing it the x and y vectors as arguments.

In summary, using Rcpp for C++ integration allows for writing high-performance algorithms for R. It provides a seamless integration between R and C++, and R developers can take advantage of C++s speed and flexibility to write high-performance code in R.

5.9   Describe methods for handling and analyzing network data in R, including packages such as igraph and network.

Network analysis is the study of graphs and networks, which are structures that consist of nodes (also known as vertices) and edges (also known as links or ties) that connect them. These structures are used to model a wide range of phenomena, such as social interactions, transportation systems, and biological networks. In R, there are several packages available for handling and analyzing network data, including igraph and network.

The igraph package provides tools for creating, manipulating, and visualizing graphs. It supports a wide range of graph types, including directed and undirected graphs, weighted graphs, and bipartite graphs. Some of the key functions in igraph include:

- graph_from_edgelist(): Creates a graph object from a list of edges.

- degree(): Computes the degree of each node in a graph.

- clustering(): Computes the clustering coefficient of each node in a graph.

- shortest_paths(): Computes the shortest path between each pair of nodes in a graph.

- plot(): Visualizes a graph using various layouts and styles.

Here's an example of creating a simple graph using igraph:

```
library(igraph)

# Create an empty graph with 5 nodes
g <- graph.empty(5)

# Add some edges to the graph
g <- add_edges(g, c(1,2,2,3,3,4,4,5))

# Visualize the graph
plot(g)
```

The network package provides a framework for handling and analyzing network data, with a focus on social network analysis. It supports a wide range of network types, including one-mode and two-mode networks, valued and binary networks, and dynamic networks. Some of the key functions in network include:

- network(): Creates a network object from a variety of input formats.

- degree(): Computes the degree of each node in a network.

- closeness(): Computes the closeness centrality of each node in a network.

- betweenness(): Computes the betweenness centrality of each node in a network.

- plot(): Visualizes a network using various layouts and styles.

Here's an example of creating a simple network using network:

```
library(network)

# Create an empty network with 5 nodes
n <- network.initialize(5)

# Add some ties to the network
n <- set.edge(n, c(1,2,2,3,3,4,4,5))

# Visualize the network
plot(n)
```

Overall, igraph and network are powerful tools for handling and analyzing network data in R, with a wide range of functions and capabilities.

5.10   Explain advanced statistical modeling techniques in R, such as Bayesian modeling and hierarchical models, using packages like rstan and brms.

Bayesian modeling and hierarchical models are advanced statistical modeling techniques that can be implemented using various R packages, including rstan and brms.

Bayesian modeling is a statistical approach that uses Bayes' theorem to model and update our beliefs about the probability of an event based on new data. It involves specifying a prior distribution and updating it with data to obtain a posterior distribution, which represents our updated belief about the probability of the event. In R, the rstan package provides a flexible platform for fitting Bayesian models using Markov chain Monte Carlo (MCMC) methods. For example, we can use rstan to fit a simple linear regression model with a normal prior distribution on the intercept and slope coefficients:

```
library(rstan)

# Define data
x <- rnorm(100)
y <- rnorm(100, mean = 2 + 3 * x, sd = 0.5)

# Define model
model <- "
   data {
      int<lower=0> N;
      vector[N] x;
      vector[N] y;
   }
   parameters {
      real alpha;
      real beta;
      real<lower=0> sigma;
   }
```

```
   model {
       y ~ normal(alpha + beta * x, sigma);
       alpha ~ normal(0, 10);
       beta ~ normal(0, 10);
       sigma ~ cauchy(0, 2.5);
   }
   "

   # Compile model
   stan_model <- stan_model(model_code = model)

   # Fit model
   stan_fit <- sampling(stan_model, data = list(N = length(x),
       x = x, y = y),
   chains = 4, iter = 2000, warmup = 1000)

   # Print summary of posterior distributions
   print(stan_fit)
```

Hierarchical models are a type of statistical model that incorporates group-level and individual-level effects. For example, we may want to model the effect of a treatment on individual patients, while also accounting for variation in the treatment effect across different hospitals. In R, the brms package provides a flexible framework for fitting hierarchical models using a Bayesian approach. For example, we can use brms to fit a hierarchical logistic regression model with random effects for intercept and slope:

```
   library(brms)

   # Load data
   data("cbpp", package = "lme4")

   # Fit hierarchical logistic regression model
   fit <- brm(
   bf(cb ~ 1 + (1 | herd) + (1 | cow)),
   data = cbpp, family = binomial(),
   chains = 4, iter = 2000, warmup = 1000
   )

   # Print summary of posterior distributions
   print(fit)
```

These are just a few examples of the advanced statistical modeling techniques that can be implemented in R using various packages. Understanding these techniques can be important for developing more sophisticated statistical models and analyses.

5.11   How do you implement advanced machine learning techniques in R, including deep learning and reinforcement learning? Provide examples using packages like keras and reinforcementlearning.

R has several powerful packages for implementing advanced machine learning techniques, including deep learning and reinforcement learning.

To implement deep learning in R, the most commonly used package is keras. It provides an interface for building and training neural networks, with support for various types of layers, activation functions, and optimization algorithms. Here's an example of how to use keras to train a simple neural network to classify handwritten digits:

```
library(keras)
mnist <- dataset_mnist()
x_train <- mnist$train$x / 255
y_train <- to_categorical(mnist$train$y)
x_test <- mnist$test$x / 255
y_test <- to_categorical(mnist$test$y)

model <- keras_model_sequential() %>%
layer_dense(units = 128, activation = 'relu', input_shape =
    c(784)) %>%
```

```
layer_dropout(rate = 0.5) %>%
layer_dense(units = 10, activation = 'softmax')

model %>% compile(
loss = 'categorical_crossentropy',
optimizer = optimizer_rmsprop(),
metrics = c('accuracy')
)

history <- model %>% fit(
x_train, y_train,
epochs = 20,
batch_size = 128,
validation_split = 0.2
)

plot(history)
```

This code downloads the MNIST dataset of handwritten digits, preprocesses the data, builds a simple neural network with two layers, trains the model using the fit() function, and plots the training history.

To implement reinforcement learning in R, the most commonly used package is reinforcementlearning. It provides a framework for building and training reinforcement learning agents that can interact with an environment and learn to optimize a reward function. Here's an example of how to use reinforcementlearning to train a simple agent to play the FrozenLake game:

```
library(reinforcementlearning)
env <- create_FrozenLake()

agent <- rl_agent(
states = env$states,
actions = env$actions,
learning_rate = 0.1,
discount_factor = 0.9,
random_action_prob = 0.1,
method = 'Q-learning'
)

train_rl(agent, env, n_episodes = 1000)
```

```
test_rl(agent, env)
```

This code creates an environment for the FrozenLake game, creates a Q-learning agent, trains the agent using the train_rl() function, and tests the agent using the test_rl() function. The agent learns to navigate the environment and optimize the reward function over the course of training.

5.12   Discuss advanced time series analysis techniques in R, such as state-space models and dynamic factor models, using packages like KFAS and dynfactor.

Time series analysis is a crucial aspect of data analysis, especially when dealing with temporal data. In R, several packages can help conduct advanced time series analysis. Two of these packages are KFAS and dynfactor.

KFAS is an R package that provides functions for state-space modeling in R. It can handle linear and nonlinear Gaussian state space models, including models with regime-switching, and can be used for filtering, smoothing, and forecasting. KFAS is particularly useful when dealing with unobserved components models and can handle missing data.

Here is an example of using the KFAS package to fit a state-space model to the Nile river dataset, which contains annual river flow measurements for the Nile river from 1871 to 1970:

```
library(KFAS)

# Load Nile dataset
data(Nile)

# Fit state-space model
nile_model <- SSModel(log(Nile) ~ SSMtrend(1,Q=0.01)+
    SSMcycle(365.25/7,type="bs"),H=0.1^2)

# Fit model with maximum likelihood
nile_fit <- fitSSM(nile_model,method="BFGS")
summary(nile_fit)
```

This code fits a state-space model to the Nile dataset using
a local linear trend component and a cyclic component with
a period of one week. The resulting model is then fit using
maximum likelihood estimation, and a summary of the model
is printed.

Another package for advanced time series analysis in R is dynfactor, which provides functions for estimating dynamic factor
models. Dynamic factor models are a popular method for analyzing time series data and can be used for forecasting, signal
extraction, and data reduction.

Here is an example of using the dynfactor package to estimate
a dynamic factor model for the US macroeconomic dataset:

```
library(dynfactor)

# Load US macro dataset
data(macro)

# Estimate dynamic factor model
macro_dfm <- dynfactor(macro, nfactors = 4, lambda = 1,
    ar_order = 1)

# Plot factor loadings
plot(macro_dfm$loadings)
```

This code estimates a dynamic factor model for the US macroeconomic dataset with four factors and a first-order autoregressive structure. The resulting model is then plotted to show the factor loadings.

5.13   Explain the process of deploying R-based solutions in production environments, including best practices and challenges.

Deploying R-based solutions in production environments involves various steps, including packaging the solution, deploying it to a server or cloud service, and integrating it into existing systems. Here are some best practices and challenges to consider when deploying R-based solutions:

Best practices:

- Create reproducible code: Ensure that the code can be reproduced in different environments with the same inputs and outputs.

- Use version control: Use version control software like Git to keep track of code changes and facilitate collaboration.

- Write robust code: Write code that can handle errors and edge cases gracefully and provide informative error messages.

- Test thoroughly: Write unit tests, integration tests, and end-to-end tests to ensure that the solution functions correctly in production.

- Automate deployment: Use automation tools like Docker and Kubernetes to automate the deployment process and ensure consistency across different environments.

Challenges:

- Scalability: Ensure that the solution can handle increasing amounts of data and traffic as usage grows.

- Security: Protect sensitive data and prevent unauthorized access to the solution and underlying systems.

- Performance: Optimize code for performance to minimize processing time and reduce server costs.

- Compatibility: Ensure that the solution is compatible with existing systems and software versions.

- Monitoring and maintenance: Set up monitoring and alerting systems to detect and resolve issues quickly and perform regular maintenance to keep the solution up-to-date and secure.

In addition to these best practices and challenges, there are several tools and platforms available for deploying R-based solutions in production, including Shiny Server, RStudio Connect, AWS Lambda, and Microsoft Azure. These platforms provide features like load balancing, scaling, and monitoring to simplify the deployment process and ensure the solution runs smoothly in production.

5.14   How do you create custom Shiny components and extend the functionality of existing Shiny widgets?

Shiny is an R package that provides a web application framework for building interactive and reactive web applications. It allows developers to create web applications without needing to know HTML, CSS, or JavaScript, and enables users to interact with the data and models created using R.

Shiny comes with many built-in widgets, such as sliders, dropdown menus, and tables, but sometimes developers may need to create their own custom widgets to meet specific requirements or to extend the functionality of existing widgets.

Creating Custom Shiny Widgets:

To create custom Shiny widgets, developers can use the HTML and JavaScript frameworks provided by Shiny. A custom widget can be created by defining an HTML template that includes the widget's structure and styles, and a JavaScript function that provides the widget's behavior and functionality.

For example, let's say we want to create a custom widget for selecting a date range using two date pickers. We can define the widget's structure and styles in an HTML template as follows:

```
<div class="date-range-widget">
<input type="text" class="start-date" placeholder="Start␣
    Date" />
<input type="text" class="end-date" placeholder="End␣Date"
    />
</div>

<style>
.date-range-widget {
```

```
        display: flex;
        justify-content: space-between;
    }
    .date-range-widget input {
        width: 45%;
    }
    </style>
```

This defines a simple widget that includes two text inputs for
selecting a start and end date, and applies some basic styling
using CSS.

Next, we can define the widget's behavior and functionality in
a JavaScript function using the Shiny JavaScript API:

```
function dateRangeWidget(el, data) {
    // Get references to the start and end date inputs
    var startDateInput = $(el).find('.start-date');
    var endDateInput = $(el).find('.end-date');

    // Initialize the date pickers
    startDateInput.datepicker();
    endDateInput.datepicker();

    // Define a function to update the data based on the
        selected dates
    function updateData() {
        var startDate = startDateInput.val();
        var endDate = endDateInput.val();
        var filteredData = data.filter(function(d) {
            return d.date >= startDate && d.date <= endDate;
        });
        Shiny.setInputValue('filtered_data', filteredData);
    }

    // Call the updateData function whenever the date
        pickers change
    startDateInput.change(updateData);
    endDateInput.change(updateData);
}
```

This JavaScript function initializes the date pickers using the
jQuery UI datepicker library, defines a function to update the

data based on the selected dates, and uses the Shiny.setInput-
Value function to update the filtered_data input whenever the
date pickers change.

To use this custom widget in a Shiny application, we can create
a new R function that calls the JavaScript function and passes
in the required data:

```
dateRangeWidget <- function(inputId, data) {
    widgetCode <- sprintf(
    'dateRangeWidget(el,␣%s)',
    jsonlite::toJSON(data)
    )
    tags$div(id = inputId, HTML(widgetCode))
}
```

This R function creates a div element with the specified inputId,
and embeds the custom widget's HTML and JavaScript code
inside it using the HTML function.

Extending Existing Shiny Widgets:

In addition to creating custom widgets, developers can also extend the functionality of existing Shiny widgets using JavaScript.
For example, let's say we want to add a tooltip to a slider widget
to display the current value when the user hovers over it.

5.15   Describe advanced techniques for data visualization in R, such as interactive and 3D visualizations, using packages like plotly and rayshader.

R is known for its rich and flexible visualization capabilities. In
addition to the built-in graphics capabilities in base R and the

popular ggplot2 package, there are several other packages available for creating advanced and interactive visualizations. Some of these packages are plotly, shiny, gganimate, and rayshader.

Here are examples of some advanced visualization techniques using plotly and rayshader:

Interactive visualizations with plotly: Plotly is a powerful package for creating interactive visualizations in R. With plotly, you can create interactive charts, maps, and dashboards that can be embedded in web pages or Shiny apps. Here's an example of creating an interactive scatter plot with plotly:

```
library(plotly)

# Create data
x <- rnorm(100)
y <- rnorm(100)

# Create plotly object
plot_ly(x = x, y = y, mode = "markers") %>%
layout(title = "Interactive Scatter Plot",
xaxis = list(title = "X-axis"),
yaxis = list(title = "Y-axis"))
```

3D visualizations with rayshader: Rayshader is a package for creating beautiful and realistic 3D visualizations of elevation data in R. Rayshader allows you to create 3D visualizations of terrain, buildings, and other structures. Here's an example of creating a 3D plot of a digital elevation model (DEM) using rayshader:

```
library(rayshader)
library(rgl)

# Load elevation data
elev_matrix <- load DEM data

# Create heightmap and plot
heightmap <- sphere_shade(elev_matrix, texture = "desert")
```

```
plot_3d(heightmap, zscale = 30, fov = 0, theta = -45, phi =
    45)
```

These are just a few examples of the advanced visualization techniques available in R. By leveraging the power of packages like plotly and rayshader, you can create highly interactive and visually stunning visualizations that can help you better understand your data.

5.16   Explain the use of Docker for creating reproducible and portable R environments.

Docker is a popular platform for creating, deploying, and running applications in containers. Containers are lightweight, standalone executable packages that include everything needed to run an application, including the code, dependencies, and system libraries. Docker allows users to create and manage containers easily, making it an ideal platform for creating reproducible and portable R environments.

In the context of R, Docker can be used to create an isolated environment that includes a specific version of R, along with all the necessary packages and dependencies required to run a particular R application. This ensures that the R code will run in the same way on any system, regardless of the underlying operating system or other software installed on the system.

To create a Docker container for an R environment, the first step is to create a Dockerfile. This is a text file that specifies the base image, along with any additional packages and dependencies that need to be installed. Here is an example of a Dockerfile for an R environment:

```
# Use the official R base image
FROM r-base:latest

# Install any additional packages
RUN apt-get update &&
apt-get install -y
libssl-dev
libcurl4-openssl-dev
libxml2-dev

# Install required R packages
RUN install.packages(c('tidyverse', 'shiny'))

# Set the working directory
WORKDIR /app

# Copy the R code to the container
COPY app.R /app/

# Expose port 3838 for Shiny app
EXPOSE 3838

# Start the Shiny app
CMD ["R", "-e", "shiny::runApp('/app/app.R', host
    ='0.0.0.0', port=3838)"]
```

In this example, the Dockerfile specifies that the container should use the latest version of the R base image, and installs additional system dependencies required for certain R packages. It then installs the tidyverse and shiny R packages, sets the working directory to /app, copies the app.R file to the container, exposes port 3838 for the Shiny app, and finally starts the Shiny app.

Once the Dockerfile has been created, it can be used to build a Docker image. This can be done using the docker build command, as follows:

```
docker build -t my-r-app .
```

This command builds a Docker image named "my-r-app" based on the Dockerfile in the current directory.

To run the R application in the Docker container, the Docker image can be started using the docker run command:

```
docker run -p 3838:3838 my-r-app
```

This command starts the Docker container from the "my-r-app" image and maps port 3838 in the container to port 3838 on the host system, allowing the Shiny app to be accessed from a web browser on the host system.

Using Docker for creating reproducible and portable R environments offers several benefits, such as easier collaboration and sharing of code, increased consistency across different systems, and simplified deployment of R applications.

5.17 How do you ensure the security and privacy of sensitive data when working with R projects? Discuss best practices and tools.

When working with sensitive data, it is essential to follow best practices to ensure the security and privacy of the data. In this context, there are several best practices and tools available to protect sensitive data while working with R projects.

One of the most important steps is to limit access to sensitive data. This can be done by storing the data in secure locations and only allowing authorized personnel to access it. In addition, it is important to use strong passwords and two-factor authentication for accessing the data.

Another important practice is to encrypt sensitive data when it is stored or transmitted. This can be done using encryption tools such as GnuPG, which can be used to encrypt files and folders. R also has built-in support for encryption using packages like openssl and digest.

It is also important to ensure that the R code used to analyze sensitive data is secure. This can be done by using secure coding practices such as input validation, proper error handling, and avoiding hard-coded passwords or other sensitive information in the code.

When working with sensitive data, it is also important to properly dispose of the data once it is no longer needed. This can be done by securely deleting data from storage devices or using tools like shred to securely erase data.

In addition to these best practices, there are several tools available to help ensure the security and privacy of sensitive data when working with R projects. For example, the R package sodium provides high-level cryptographic functions for secure data storage and communication. The R package s2 provides secure serialization of R objects, allowing sensitive data to be stored and transmitted securely. There are also various tools available for secure data transfer and storage, such as SFTP and encrypted cloud storage solutions.

Overall, when working with sensitive data in R projects, it is important to follow best practices for data security and privacy and to use tools that are specifically designed for handling sensitive data.

5.18   Discuss advanced text mining techniques in R, such as topic modeling and sentiment analysis, using packages like stm and syuzhet.

Advanced text mining techniques in R allow us to extract deeper insights from text data. Two important techniques are topic modeling and sentiment analysis.

Topic modeling is an unsupervised learning technique that involves discovering hidden themes or topics within a set of documents. One popular algorithm for topic modeling is Latent Dirichlet Allocation (LDA). The stm package in R provides a comprehensive framework for fitting and visualizing LDA models. The package also allows us to incorporate covariates into the model to explore how different variables may affect the topic distribution.

Here's an example of fitting an LDA model using the stm package:

```
library(stm)

# Load data
data("news")
doclist <- news$content

# Create document-term matrix
processed <- textProcessor(doclist, metadata = news)
out <- prepDocuments(processed$documents, processed$vocab,
    lower.thresh = 5)

# Fit LDA model
K <- 10 # number of topics
lda <- stm(out$documents, out$vocab, K = K, init.type = "
    Spectral")

# Explore topics
```

```
plotModels(lda, type = "topic", topics = 1:K)
```

Sentiment analysis is a technique for quantifying the emotional tone of a piece of text. The syuzhet package in R provides several sentiment analysis algorithms, including the AFINN and NRC lexicons. The package allows us to calculate sentiment scores for individual words or entire documents.

Here's an example of performing sentiment analysis using the syuzhet package:

```
library(syuzhet)

# Load data
data("inaugTexts")
doclist <- inaugTexts$text

# Calculate sentiment scores
sentiment <- get_nrc_sentiment(doclist)

# Visualize sentiment over time
library(ggplot2)
library(reshape2)

sentiment_df <- data.frame(sentiment, year =
    inaugTexts$year)
sentiment_melted <- melt(sentiment_df, id.vars = "year",
    variable.name = "sentiment")
ggplot(sentiment_melted, aes(x = year, y = value, color =
    sentiment)) +
geom_line() +
ggtitle("Sentiment⎵in⎵Presidential⎵Inauguration⎵Speeches")
```

Advanced text mining techniques like topic modeling and sentiment analysis can provide deeper insights into text data and help us understand the underlying patterns and themes.

## 5.19	Explain advanced techniques for working with API endpoints in R, including authentication and rate limiting, using packages like httr and ratelimiter.

Working with API endpoints is a common task in data science, and R provides several packages to handle this task, such as httr and RCurl. In this context, advanced techniques are those that go beyond basic API requests, which include tasks such as authentication, rate limiting, and dealing with complex API structures.

One of the primary challenges when working with APIs is to ensure that only authorized users can access sensitive data. API authentication is a process of verifying the identity of the user making the request. Authentication methods can vary from API to API, but some of the most common ones include OAuth, API keys, and HTTP basic authentication. The httr package provides functions to handle all these methods of authentication. Here is an example of how to use httr to authenticate with an API using OAuth:

```
library(httr)

oauth_app <- oauth_app("my_app_name", key = "my_key",
    secret = "my_secret")
token <- oauth2.0_token(oauth_endpoints("my_api_url"),
    oauth_app)

response <- GET("my_api_url/resource", config(token = token
    ))
```

Rate limiting is another critical issue when working with APIs. API providers often limit the number of requests that can be

made per time unit to prevent overloading the server. To handle
rate limiting, we can use the ratelimiter package. Here's an
example of how to use the package to control the rate of API
requests:

```
library(ratelimiter)

api_call <- function() {
    # API call code here
}

limiter <- RateLimiter$new(api_call, rate_limit = 10,
    time_unit = "sec")
result <- limiter$run()
```

The above code defines an API call function and creates a Rate-
Limiter object that limits the function to 10 calls per second.

Finally, some APIs can have complex structures, such as nested
JSON objects or multiple endpoints that need to be called in
a particular sequence. In such cases, it may be necessary to
use advanced parsing and processing techniques. The jsonlite
package provides functions to parse JSON data, while the purrr
package offers functions to work with complex data structures.
Here's an example of how to use purrr to extract data from a
nested JSON object:

```
library(httr)
library(jsonlite)
library(purrr)

response <- GET("my_api_url/resource")
json_data <- content(response, "text")
parsed_data <- fromJSON(json_data)

result <- parsed_data %>%
map_df(function(x) {
    data.frame(a = x$a, b = x$b)
})
```

The above code sends a GET request to the API endpoint,

parses the returned JSON data, and uses purrr to extract the "a" and "b" fields from the nested object. The resulting data frame can be used for further analysis.

5.20   Describe methods for integrating R with other programming languages and platforms, such as Python and Spark, using packages like reticulate and sparklyr.

R is a powerful language for statistical computing and data analysis, but sometimes it may be necessary to integrate R with other programming languages or platforms. This allows developers to leverage the strengths of each language or platform, and to build more complex and scalable applications. In this regard, R provides various packages for integrating with other languages and platforms, including Python and Apache Spark.

The following are some examples of packages for integrating R with other languages and platforms:

reticulate: This is an R package that provides a comprehensive set of tools for interoperability between Python and R. With reticulate, R programmers can call Python code directly from within R, and vice versa. This enables R programmers to leverage the strengths of Python, such as machine learning and deep learning libraries, while staying within the R environment. For example, the following R code imports the popular scikit-learn library from Python and uses it to build a random forest model:

```
library(reticulate)
sklearn <- import("sklearn")
```

```
model <- sklearn$ensemble$RandomForestClassifier()
```

rJava: This is an R package that provides a bridge between R and Java, enabling R to interact with Java libraries and applications. With rJava, R programmers can use Java libraries for advanced analytics and data processing, while staying within the R environment. For example, the following R code creates a new Java object and invokes a method from the java.util package: scss Copy code library(rJava) .jinit() list1 <- new("java/util/ArrayList") list1$add("Hello") list1$add("World")

sparklyr: This is an R package that provides a convenient interface to Apache Spark, a popular distributed computing platform. With sparklyr, R programmers can interact with Spark DataFrames and manipulate large datasets using Spark's distributed computing capabilities. For example, the following R code connects to a Spark cluster and performs a basic analysis on a dataset:

```
library(sparklyr)
sc <- spark_connect(master = "local")
df <- spark_read_csv(sc, "path/to/data.csv")
summary(df)
```

Overall, the integration of R with other programming languages and platforms enables developers to build more powerful and scalable applications that leverage the strengths of multiple technologies.

Chapter 6

Guru

6.1 Discuss the role of R in the broader landscape of data science and statistical programming languages. Compare and contrast R with other languages like Python and Julia.

R is a widely-used programming language and environment for statistical computing and graphics. It is open-source, free, and has a large and active community of users and developers. R has become one of the most popular languages for data analysis, modeling, and visualization, with a rich set of built-in functions and a vast collection of user-contributed packages.

Python is another popular language for data science and machine learning, with a similar level of popularity as R. Python has a more general-purpose focus, with a wider range of applications beyond statistical analysis. Python is also known for its ease of use and readability, with a large community and ecosystem of libraries and tools.

Julia is a newer language that is gaining popularity in the data science community. It is designed to be fast, efficient, and easy to use, with a syntax that is similar to that of MATLAB and Python. Julia is particularly well-suited for scientific computing and numerical analysis, with built-in support for parallel and distributed computing.

While each language has its strengths and weaknesses, the choice of language often depends on the specific needs and preferences of the user or organization. R is often preferred for its ease of use and built-in statistical functions, Python for its versatility and wide range of applications, and Julia for its speed and efficiency. Ultimately, the best language for a given project depends on factors such as the size and complexity of the data, the nature of the analysis or modeling, and the skills and preferences of the team members involved.

6.2   Explain how to design and implement custom domain-specific languages (DSLs) in R for specialized use cases.

Domain-specific languages (DSLs) are programming languages designed for a specific domain or task. In R, DSLs can be created using a combination of language features and packages that allow for the creation of custom syntax and semantics for a specific domain.

One approach to creating DSLs in R is to use the magrittr
package, which provides the %>% pipe operator for creating a
fluent interface. The pipe operator allows for the creation of a
DSL that resembles natural language, making it easier for domain experts to understand and use. For example, the following
code shows a DSL for filtering and summarizing data:

```
library(dplyr)
library(magrittr)

mydsl <- function(data) {
   data %>%
   filter(Sepal.Length > 5) %>%
   group_by(Species) %>%
   summarize(mean = mean(Petal.Length))
}

iris %>% mydsl()
```

Another approach to creating DSLs in R is to use the parser
package, which allows for the creation of custom parsers and
grammars. This package provides tools for building a lexer,
parser, and AST (Abstract Syntax Tree) for a DSL. The resulting parser can be used to create custom syntax and semantics
for a specific domain. For example, the following code shows a
simple DSL for working with vectors:

```
library(parser)

mydsl <- function(expr) {
   parser <- Parser(grammar = list(
   expr <- expression,
   expression <- vector_expr,
   vector_expr <- '[' numeric_expr (',' numeric_expr)* ']',
   numeric_expr <- '1'..'9' '0'..'9'*
   ))

   ast <- parser$parse(expr)

   if (length(ast) == 1 && is.numeric(ast[[1]])) {
      return(ast[[1]])
   } else {
      stop("Invalid␣expression")
```

```
      }
    }
  mydsl("[1,␣2,␣3]")
```

In this example, the DSL allows for the creation of a vector expression using square brackets. The resulting AST can be used to evaluate the expression and return the resulting vector.

Overall, creating custom DSLs in R can be a powerful tool for simplifying and streamlining domain-specific tasks. The approach used will depend on the specific requirements of the domain and the level of customization needed.

6.3   Describe the challenges and best practices for scaling R-based solutions in large organizations and complex systems.

As an open-source language, R has gained popularity due to its flexibility and wide range of packages for statistical computing, machine learning, and data visualization. However, when it comes to scaling R-based solutions in large organizations and complex systems, certain challenges arise. Here are some of the challenges and best practices for scaling R-based solutions.

Challenges

Performance and memory limitations: R is a memory-bound language, and its performance can be slower when dealing with large datasets. Also, the language has limitations in handling parallelism, which makes it challenging to scale R-based solutions.

Version control and reproducibility: Ensuring reproducibility and version control in R-based solutions can be challenging, especially when working with multiple teams or data scientists.

Integration with other technologies: R is often used as part of a larger system or technology stack, which can present challenges in terms of integration with other tools and platforms.

Maintaining code quality: As R-based solutions grow in size and complexity, it can be challenging to maintain code quality and adhere to coding best practices.

Best Practices

Optimizing performance: To optimize performance in R-based solutions, consider using more efficient packages like data.table or ff, or using parallel processing techniques like the future package.

Establishing standards and guidelines: To ensure version control and reproducibility, establish standards and guidelines for coding, naming conventions, and documentation. This helps to maintain consistency across the organization and ensure that R-based solutions can be reproduced easily.

Collaboration and communication: Establish clear communication channels and collaboration processes between data scientists, analysts, and IT teams. This helps to ensure that R-based solutions can be integrated with other technologies and platforms.

Testing and validation: Implement testing and validation processes for R-based solutions to ensure that code quality is maintained and errors are caught early.

Continuous integration and deployment: Implement continuous integration and deployment (CI/CD) practices to ensure that R-based solutions are tested and deployed quickly and efficiently. Tools like GitHub Actions and Travis CI can be used to automate the testing and deployment process.

Training and education: Provide training and education for data scientists, analysts, and IT teams to ensure that they have the necessary skills and knowledge to work with R-based solutions effectively.

Leverage the R community: Leverage the R community to stay up-to-date with the latest packages, best practices, and techniques for scaling R-based solutions. Attend conferences, participate in forums, and engage with other R users to learn from their experiences and share knowledge.

In conclusion, scaling R-based solutions in large organizations and complex systems requires careful consideration of performance limitations, version control, integration with other technologies, and maintaining code quality. By following best practices such as optimizing performance, establishing standards and guidelines, and implementing testing and validation processes, organizations can ensure that their R-based solutions can be scaled effectively and efficiently.

6.4 Discuss advanced statistical theory and its application in R, including topics such as asymptotic analysis, nonparametric methods, and causal inference.

Advanced statistical theory plays a crucial role in the development of statistical methods and models. In R, there are many packages that provide implementations of advanced statistical methods, such as asymptotic analysis, non-parametric methods, and causal inference. Here, we will briefly discuss each of these topics and provide some examples of how to implement them in R.

Asymptotic analysis: Asymptotic analysis involves the study of the behavior of statistical methods as the sample size grows infinitely large. This is important because many statistical methods rely on asymptotic properties to make inferences about the population. In R, the asymptotic analysis can be done using various packages, such as stats, MASS, and asymptotics. For example, to compute the asymptotic standard error for the mean, we can use the following code:

```
library(MASS)
data <- rnorm(100)
se <- sqrt(var(data)/100)
```

Non-parametric methods: Non-parametric methods are statistical techniques that do not rely on specific assumptions about the underlying distribution of the data. This makes them particularly useful when dealing with data that does not meet the assumptions of traditional parametric methods. In R, there are many packages that provide non-parametric methods, such

as bootstrap, nortest, and locfit. For example, to perform
a Wilcoxon signed-rank test in R, we can use the following
code: kotlin Copy code data <- c(1, 2, 3, 4, 5, 6, 7, 8, 9, 10)
wilcox.test(data, mu = 5, alternative = "greater")

Causal inference: Causal inference is the process of drawing
conclusions about causal relationships between variables. It is
an important topic in many fields, including epidemiology, economics, and social sciences. In R, there are many packages that
provide tools for causal inference, such as causaleffect, matching, and propensity. For example, to estimate the average treatment effect using propensity score matching in R, we can use
the following code:

```
library(Matching)
data(lalonde)
m.out <- Match(Y = lalonde$re78, Tr = lalonde$treat, X =
    lalonde[, -c(1:2)])
summary(m.out)
```

In summary, advanced statistical theory is an important part
of statistical programming in R. The packages available in R
provide a wide range of tools to implement and apply advanced
statistical methods in real-world situations.

6.5 Explain how to develop and maintain high-quality, performant, and stable R packages that address the needs of a specific domain or industry.

Developing and maintaining high-quality, performant, and stable R packages that address the needs of a specific domain or

industry requires a strong understanding of both the programming language and the target domain. In this answer, we will discuss the best practices and considerations for developing such packages.

Identify the Needs and Goals

The first step in developing an R package for a specific domain or industry is to identify the needs and goals of the users. This involves conducting a thorough analysis of the domain or industry and determining what functions, algorithms, and methods are required to meet the needs of the users. This analysis should also include an understanding of the current tools and technologies used in the domain or industry, as well as any limitations or challenges that may arise.

Follow Best Practices for Package Development

Once the needs and goals of the users have been identified, it is important to follow best practices for package development to ensure the package is high-quality, performant, and stable. This includes:

Writing clear and concise documentation: Good documentation is essential for users to understand how to use the package and what it can do. This includes documenting functions, arguments, return values, and examples of usage.

Writing test cases: Test cases help ensure the package functions as expected and can help catch bugs and errors. Unit tests should be written for each function in the package, and integration tests should be written to test the package as a whole.

Maintaining version control: Version control is essential for tracking changes to the package over time and ensuring the package remains stable. A version control system such as Git should be used, and version numbers should be incremented for each release.

Following coding standards: Code should be written to follow best practices for coding standards, including formatting, naming conventions, and code structure.

Optimize Performance

To ensure the package is performant, it is important to optimize the code for speed and efficiency. This includes:

Avoiding unnecessary computations: Unnecessary computations should be avoided to reduce computation time and memory usage. This includes removing redundant computations, precomputing values, and optimizing loops.

Using data structures and algorithms optimized for performance: The choice of data structures and algorithms can have a significant impact on performance. Where possible, data structures and algorithms optimized for performance should be used.

Parallelizing computations: Parallelization can be used to distribute computations across multiple cores or nodes, which can significantly improve performance for large datasets or complex computations.

Ensure Compatibility and Usability

To ensure the package is usable by a wide range of users, it is important to ensure compatibility with different versions of R, different operating systems, and different hardware configurations. This includes:

Testing on multiple platforms: The package should be tested on different platforms, including different versions of R, different operating systems, and different hardware configurations.

Providing clear error messages: Clear and concise error messages should be provided to help users understand what went wrong and how to fix it.

Providing examples and tutorials: Examples and tutorials should be provided to help users understand how to use the package and what it can do.

Conclusion

Developing and maintaining high-quality, performant, and stable R packages that address the needs of a specific domain or industry requires a strong understanding of both the programming language and the target domain. By following best practices for package development, optimizing performance, and ensuring compatibility and usability, R packages can be developed that meet the needs of users in a wide range of domains and industries.

6.6   Describe the role of R in the development of cutting-edge algorithms and models in fields such as artificial intelligence, network science, and bioinformatics.

R is a widely used language for statistical computing, data analysis, and machine learning. It has become a go-to tool for data scientists and researchers in various domains, including artificial intelligence, network science, and bioinformatics. R has a vast array of packages and libraries that provide powerful tools for implementing cutting-edge algorithms and models in these fields.

In artificial intelligence, R is widely used for developing machine learning algorithms such as decision trees, random forests, and neural networks. Packages such as caret, keras, and mxnet provide a range of tools for building and training machine learning models in R. With the growing popularity of deep learning, R has also developed a robust ecosystem of packages for implementing advanced deep learning architectures such as convolutional neural networks (CNNs) and recurrent neural networks (RNNs).

In network science, R provides a range of packages for analyzing and visualizing complex networks. Packages such as igraph and network provide a range of tools for working with networks and graph data, including algorithms for network analysis, visualization, and clustering.

In bioinformatics, R has become a critical tool for analyzing genomic data and performing statistical analysis on biological data. R packages such as Bioconductor provide a range of tools for analyzing and visualizing genomic data, including tools for gene expression analysis, sequence analysis, and pathway analysis. R is also widely used for developing statistical models in the field of epidemiology, such as models for predicting disease outbreaks and analyzing the spread of infectious diseases.

Overall, R has become a key player in the development and application of cutting-edge algorithms and models in fields such as artificial intelligence, network science, and bioinformatics, pro-

viding researchers and practitioners with a powerful and flexible
tool for data analysis, modeling, and visualization.

6.7   Discuss the state-of-the-art in R-based data visualization, including innovative techniques and research in the field.

R has a rich ecosystem of data visualization packages, with
many innovative techniques and research being developed to improve the quality and effectiveness of data visualizations. Some
of the state-of-the-art techniques in R-based data visualization
include:

Interactive visualizations: Interactive visualizations allow users
to explore and manipulate data in real-time, making it easier to
identify patterns and trends. The plotly package is a popular
choice for creating interactive visualizations in R, and allows
for the creation of interactive plots, charts, and dashboards.

```
library(plotly)

# Create an interactive scatter plot
plot_ly(mtcars, x = ~wt, y = ~mpg, color = ~cyl, size = ~hp
        ,
text = ~paste("Model:", rownames(mtcars))) %>%
add_markers() %>%
layout(title = "Interactive Scatter Plot")
```

3D visualizations: 3D visualizations can help to represent complex data in a more intuitive way. The rgl package is a popular
choice for creating 3D visualizations in R, and allows for the
creation of interactive 3D plots and animations.

```
library(rgl)
```

```
# Create a 3D scatter plot
plot3d(mtcars[,1:3], col=mtcars$cyl)

# Create a 3D surface plot
z <- volcano
surface3d(x=1:nrow(z), y=1:ncol(z), z=z, col=topo.colors
    (100), alpha=0.8)
```

Network visualization: Network visualization techniques are used to represent relationships between entities. The igraph package is a popular choice for creating network visualizations in R, and allows for the creation of interactive network graphs and tree diagrams.

```
library(igraph)

# Create a network graph
g <- sample_gnm(10, 15)
plot(g, vertex.color="red", vertex.size=30, edge.color="
    black", edge.width=2)

# Create a tree diagram
library(dendextend)
hc <- hclust(dist(USArrests), "ave")
dend <- as.dendrogram(hc)
plot(dend)
```

Visualizing uncertainty: Many data visualizations fail to represent the uncertainty in the underlying data. The ggplot2 package includes several techniques for representing uncertainty, such as error bars, confidence intervals, and shading.

```
library(ggplot2)

# Create a scatter plot with error bars
ggplot(mtcars, aes(x=wt, y=mpg)) +
geom_point() +
geom_errorbar(aes(ymin=mpg-1, ymax=mpg+1), width=0.1)

# Create a bar plot with confidence intervals
ggplot(mpg, aes(x=class, y=hwy)) +
geom_bar(stat="summary", fun.y=mean) +
geom_errorbar(stat="summary", fun.data=mean_cl_normal)
```

In addition to these techniques, researchers are also developing new methods for representing uncertainty, using machine learning algorithms for data visualization, and exploring the use of virtual and augmented reality for data visualization.

6.8 Explain the use of R in the development of advanced statistical models for social science, economics, and public policy.

R is widely used for developing advanced statistical models in social science, economics, and public policy. R provides a wide range of statistical and econometric packages that enable researchers and analysts to model complex data, explore relationships between variables, and test hypotheses. In this context, R is used for data analysis, model estimation, inference, and visualization.

R provides packages such as plm for panel data analysis, AER for applied econometrics, lme4 for linear mixed-effects models, and survival for survival analysis. These packages enable researchers to model complex relationships between variables, control for unobserved heterogeneity, estimate treatment effects, and analyze survival data.

R also provides packages for conducting causal inference, including causality and Matching. These packages enable researchers to identify causal relationships between variables and estimate treatment effects using techniques such as propensity score matching, instrumental variables, and difference-in-differences.

In public policy, R is used to model and analyze the impact of policies on different outcomes, such as health, education, and income. R provides packages such as lavaan for structural equation modeling, OpenBUGS and JAGS for Bayesian modeling, and glmnet for regularized regression. These packages enable researchers to estimate the impact of policies on different outcomes, control for confounding factors, and make predictions about future outcomes.

Overall, R's wide range of statistical and econometric packages make it a powerful tool for developing and applying advanced models in social science, economics, and public policy. The ability to easily share and reproduce code and results also makes R a valuable tool for promoting transparency and reproducibility in research.

6.9   Describe the role of R in the analysis and modeling of complex systems, such as ecological, financial, or transportation systems.

R is a powerful tool for the analysis and modeling of complex systems in a wide range of fields, including ecology, finance, transportation, and more. R provides a flexible and comprehensive suite of tools for data analysis, statistical modeling, and visualization, making it well-suited for handling the complexities of these systems.

One important feature of R that makes it particularly useful for modeling complex systems is its support for advanced statistical modeling techniques, including machine learning, time series

analysis, and Bayesian modeling. These techniques allow for
the development of sophisticated models that can capture the
intricate relationships and patterns within complex systems.

For example, in ecology, R has been used to model the dynamics
of ecosystems and populations, such as predator-prey relationships, species interactions, and nutrient cycling. The package
"vegan" provides tools for multivariate analysis of ecological
communities, while "adehabitat" allows for analysis of animal
movement and habitat selection.

In finance, R has been used for a variety of tasks, including
risk management, portfolio optimization, and trading strategy
development. The "quantmod" package provides tools for financial modeling and analysis, while "xts" and "zoo" allow for
the manipulation and analysis of time series data.

In transportation, R has been used to model traffic flow, optimize transportation systems, and analyze travel behavior. The
"STplanr" package provides tools for spatial and transport plan-
ning, while "spatialreg" allows for spatial modeling and analysis.

Overall, the flexibility and power of R make it a valuable tool
for the analysis and modeling of complex systems in a wide
range of fields. By using R, researchers and practitioners can
gain insights into the behavior of these systems and develop
effective strategies for managing them.

6.10   Discuss the use of R in the development of advanced machine learning models for image, audio, and video processing.

R has gained popularity in recent years due to its wide range of machine learning packages that support various advanced techniques for image, audio, and video processing. In this context, R has been used in the development of deep learning models, such as convolutional neural networks (CNNs), recurrent neural networks (RNNs), and generative adversarial networks (GANs), among others.

One of the most popular packages for deep learning in R is Keras, which provides a high-level interface to the TensorFlow backend. With Keras, users can easily build and train deep learning models for image classification, object detection, and other tasks. For example, the following code snippet demonstrates how to build a simple CNN model for image classification:

```
library(keras)

# Define the model architecture
model <- keras_model_sequential() %>%
layer_conv_2d(filters = 32, kernel_size = c(3, 3),
    activation = "relu", input_shape = c(28, 28, 1)) %>%
layer_max_pooling_2d(pool_size = c(2, 2)) %>%
layer_flatten() %>%
layer_dense(units = 128, activation = "relu") %>%
layer_dropout(rate = 0.5) %>%
layer_dense(units = 10, activation = "softmax")

# Compile the model
model %>% compile(
loss = "categorical_crossentropy",
optimizer = optimizer_adam(lr = 0.001),
metrics = c("accuracy")
```

```
)

# Train the model
model %>% fit(
x_train, y_train,
epochs = 10,
batch_size = 128,
validation_split = 0.2
)

# Evaluate the model on the test set
model %>% evaluate(x_test, y_test)
```

In addition to Keras, R provides other packages for image and video processing, such as magick, imager, and vidger. These packages allow users to read, manipulate, and analyze images and videos, as well as extract features from them for use in machine learning models.

For audio processing, the tuneR package provides functions for reading, manipulating, and analyzing audio files, as well as extracting features such as pitch and spectrograms. The sound package provides functions for generating and playing sounds, as well as performing frequency analysis and filtering.

Overall, R offers a wide range of packages and tools for advanced machine learning and signal processing in various domains, including image, audio, and video processing.

6.11   Explain the role of R in addressing ethical and social implications of data science, such as fairness, accountability, and transparency in algorithm design and deployment.

R has a crucial role to play in addressing ethical and social implications of data science. As data science and machine learning techniques are increasingly being used to make decisions that affect people's lives, it is essential to ensure that these algorithms are transparent, accountable, and fair. R provides various packages and tools for implementing ethical and socially responsible data science practices.

One of the essential aspects of ethical data science is fairness. R packages like fairmodels and fairml can be used to detect and mitigate bias in models. These packages provide various methods for assessing and correcting bias in models, such as pre-processing, in-processing, and post-processing techniques.

Another important aspect is accountability, which is about ensuring that decisions made by algorithms are transparent and explainable. R packages like DALEX and explainR provide methods for model interpretation and visualization, making it easier to understand how the model makes predictions. These packages allow users to explore the factors that drive model predictions and provide explanations for specific outcomes.

Transparency is also crucial for ethical data science. R packages like auditor and iml provide methods for auditing models, allowing users to understand how models are constructed and the factors that influence their predictions. These packages also provide ways to visualize the model's behavior, allowing users to identify any unexpected patterns or behaviors.

Finally, R has a vital role to play in promoting ethical and socially responsible data science practices. Packages like ethics, tidyethics, and AI Ethics provide tools and frameworks for ethical decision-making, making it easier for data scientists to incorporate ethical considerations into their work.

In conclusion, R provides various packages and tools that can be used to address the ethical and social implications of data science. By incorporating these practices into their workflows, data scientists can help ensure that their models are transparent, accountable, and fair.

6.12 Describe the use of R in the development of custom tools for data-driven decision-making and optimization in specific industries or domains.

R is a versatile programming language for data science and statistical computing, widely used across industries and domains. One of the strengths of R is its flexibility and extensibility, allowing users to develop custom tools and packages that address specific needs and requirements.

In the context of data-driven decision-making and optimization, R can be used to develop custom tools and models for a wide range of industries and domains, including finance, marketing, healthcare, transportation, energy, and more. Some examples of R-based applications in these domains include:

Financial risk management: R can be used to develop models and algorithms for risk assessment, portfolio optimization, and fraud detection in finance. The package "quantmod" provides a suite of tools for financial modeling and analysis, while "rugarch" offers advanced tools for modeling and forecasting financial time series.

Marketing and customer analytics: R can be used to develop models and algorithms for customer segmentation, churn prediction, and marketing campaign optimization. The package "caret" provides a wide range of tools for machine learning and predictive modeling, while "ggplot2" offers powerful tools for data visualization and communication.

Healthcare analytics: R can be used to develop models and algorithms for patient risk assessment, disease detection, and treatment optimization in healthcare. The package "mlr" provides a suite of tools for machine learning and predictive modeling, while "survival" offers advanced tools for survival analysis and event prediction.

Transportation and logistics optimization: R can be used to develop models and algorithms for route optimization, fleet management, and supply chain optimization in transportation and logistics. The package "lpSolve" provides tools for linear and integer programming, while "simmer" offers tools for discrete event simulation and optimization.

In all of these domains, the flexibility and extensibility of R allow users to develop custom tools and models that address specific needs and requirements. R's open-source community also provides a wealth of resources and packages that can be leveraged to accelerate development and reduce development costs.

Overall, R's role in the development of custom tools for data-driven decision-making and optimization is critical, as it enables organizations and industries to leverage data and analytics to improve performance, reduce costs, and drive innovation.

6.13 Discuss the role of R in the analysis of large-scale, high-dimensional, and streaming data, including the development of advanced algorithms and models for big data.

R has been widely used in the analysis of large-scale, high-dimensional, and streaming data. The development of advanced algorithms and models for big data has been facilitated by the extensive set of packages in R.

One package that is widely used for big data analysis is the dplyr package. This package provides a set of functions for data manipulation and transformation that are optimized for performance on large datasets. The dplyr package is designed to work with data stored in memory, and can handle datasets with millions of rows and thousands of columns.

Another popular package for big data analysis is data.table. This package is designed to work with very large datasets that may not fit in memory. It provides a set of functions for efficient data manipulation and transformation, and uses memory-mapped files to optimize performance. data.table is known for its fast and efficient performance, and is widely used in industry for big data analysis.

The ff package is another package that is used for working with
large datasets that do not fit in memory. This package uses
file-backed data structures to store data on disk, and provides
a set of functions for manipulating and transforming this data.
The ff package is designed to work with datasets that are too
large to fit in memory, and is optimized for performance on very
large datasets.

For analyzing high-dimensional data, packages such as tidyverse, tidyr, and ggplot2 can be used for efficient data manipulation and visualization. These packages offer tools for tidying and reshaping data, making it easier to work with high-
dimensional data in R.

In addition, packages like sparklyr and rhipe enable users to
work with distributed computing platforms like Apache Spark
and Hadoop, respectively. These packages provide an interface
to these platforms from within R, allowing users to analyze
large-scale data using R programming language.

Overall, R has proven to be a powerful tool for analyzing large-
scale, high-dimensional, and streaming data. Its wide range of
packages and tools, as well as its open-source nature, make it
a popular choice for data scientists and analysts working with
big data.

6.14 Explain the use of R in addressing the challenges of reproducibility, provenance, and data management in data science.

Reproducibility, provenance, and data management are important aspects of data science, as they ensure that research results are reliable, trustworthy, and can be verified and built upon by other researchers. R offers a range of tools and techniques for addressing these challenges, including version control, data annotation, workflow management, and documentation.

One of the most popular tools for managing reproducibility in R is the RStudio IDE, which provides an integrated environment for managing R projects and version control through Git. RStudio also includes tools for tracking changes, managing dependencies, and generating reports and documentation, making it easy to maintain a complete record of the data and analysis process.

Another important tool for managing reproducibility in R is the packrat package, which allows users to create a self-contained package library for their projects. This ensures that all dependencies are included in the project, making it easy to reproduce the analysis on different machines or environments.

Provenance is another important aspect of data science, as it allows researchers to track the origin and transformation of data, as well as the steps taken to arrive at specific results. One tool for capturing provenance in R is the data provenance package, which allows users to annotate data sets with information about their origin, format, and processing steps.

Data management is another critical aspect of data science, as it ensures that data is accurate, consistent, and properly formatted. R offers a range of tools for data management, including packages for data cleaning and transformation, such as dplyr and tidyr, as well as packages for working with different data formats, such as readr and haven.

Overall, R offers a comprehensive set of tools for addressing the challenges of reproducibility, provenance, and data management in data science. By leveraging these tools and best practices, researchers can ensure that their results are reliable, trustworthy, and can be easily replicated and built upon by others.

6.15   Describe the role of R in the development of advanced tools and platforms for data collaboration, data sharing, and data publishing.

R plays a critical role in the development of advanced tools and platforms for data collaboration, data sharing, and data publishing. It is widely used in the research community to share data and code, and as a language for scientific computing, R has a rich ecosystem of tools and packages that support reproducible research and data sharing.

One example of an R-based tool for data collaboration and sharing is the RStudio Connect platform. RStudio Connect allows users to publish and share interactive R applications, Shiny apps, and R Markdown documents with a wider audience. It provides a secure and scalable environment for hosting R-based content, making it easy to share and collaborate on data and code.

Another example is the ROpenSci project, which provides a suite of R packages for accessing and working with a wide range of scientific data sources. The project is dedicated to creating tools and infrastructure for data sharing and collaboration in the scientific community, and its packages cover a diverse range of fields, including ecology, genomics, and climate science.

R also has a strong presence in the world of open data and open science. The Open Data Science Conference (ODSC) is an example of a conference that brings together researchers, developers, and practitioners from a wide range of fields to discuss the latest developments in open data and open science. The R community is well-represented at this conference, and many of the talks and workshops focus on using R to collaborate on and share data.

Finally, R is increasingly being used as a language for developing data-driven web applications and platforms. For example, the OpenCPU project provides a platform for developing and deploying R-based APIs and web applications, making it easy to integrate R-based analysis and visualization into other applications and workflows.

Overall, R plays a key role in the development of advanced tools and platforms for data collaboration, data sharing, and data publishing. Its strong community and rich ecosystem of packages and tools make it a powerful language for reproducible research and data-driven innovation.

6.16   Discuss the use of R in the analysis and modeling of complex networks, such as social networks, biological networks, and the World Wide Web.

R is a powerful tool for analyzing and modeling complex networks, such as social networks, biological networks, and the World Wide Web. There are several packages in R that can be used for network analysis, including igraph, network, and statnet.

The igraph package provides tools for creating and analyzing graphs, including measures of centrality, clustering, and community structure. For example, the following code creates a graph using igraph and calculates the betweenness centrality of each node:

```
library(igraph)

# Create a graph
g <- make_ring(10)

# Calculate betweenness centrality
betweenness(g)
```

The network package provides similar functionality, as well as tools for visualization and statistical modeling of networks. For example, the following code creates a network object and visualizes it using the Fruchterman-Reingold layout algorithm:

```
library(network)

# Create a network object
net <- network(cbind(c(1,1,2,3,3), c(2,3,3,4,5)))

# Plot the network
```

```
plot(net, layout=fruchterman.reingold)
```

The statnet package provides tools for fitting statistical models to network data, such as exponential random graph models (ERGMs) and stochastic actor-oriented models (SAOMs). For example, the following code fits an ERGM to a network object and extracts the coefficients:

```
library(statnet)

# Fit an ERGM to the network
fit <- ergm(net ~ edges)

# Extract the coefficients
coef(fit)
```

Overall, R provides a powerful and flexible platform for analyzing and modeling complex networks, with a variety of tools and packages available for different types of analysis and modeling.

6.17   Explain the role of R in the development of advanced models for natural language processing, text mining, and computational linguistics.

R is a popular programming language for natural language processing (NLP) and text mining. It offers several packages that provide a wide range of functionalities for text processing, such as tokenization, stemming, stopword removal, sentiment analysis, topic modeling, and machine translation. In this answer, we will discuss the role of R in the development of advanced models for NLP and text mining.

One of the most popular packages for text mining in R is
the tm package, which provides a framework for handling and
manipulating text data. The tm package offers functions for
text preprocessing, such as removing punctuation, stop words,
and numbers, stemming and lemmatization, and creating a
document-term matrix for further analysis. Here is an example
of how to use the tm package to preprocess text data:

```
library(tm)
# load text data
text_data <- c("This␣is␣an␣example␣sentence.", "Here␣is␣
    another␣example␣sentence.")

# create corpus object
text_corpus <- Corpus(VectorSource(text_data))

# preprocess text
text_corpus <- tm_map(text_corpus, tolower)
text_corpus <- tm_map(text_corpus, removePunctuation)
text_corpus <- tm_map(text_corpus, removeNumbers)
text_corpus <- tm_map(text_corpus, removeWords, stopwords("
    english"))
text_corpus <- tm_map(text_corpus, stemDocument)

# create document-term matrix
dtm <- DocumentTermMatrix(text_corpus)
```

Another popular package for text mining in R is the tidytext
package, which provides tools for tidy data principles to text
analysis. The tidytext package offers functions for tokenization,
unnesting and manipulation of text data, and sentiment analysis. Here is an example of how to use the tidytext package to
analyze sentiment in text data:

```
library(tidytext)
# load text data
text_data <- data.frame(text = c("This␣is␣a␣positive␣
    sentence.", "This␣is␣a␣negative␣sentence."))

# tokenize text
text_data_tokens <- text_data %>%
unnest_tokens(word, text)
```

```
# calculate sentiment
text_data_sentiment <- text_data_tokens %>%
inner_join(get_sentiments("afinn")) %>%
group_by(text) %>%
summarize(sentiment = sum(value))
```

Moreover, the quanteda package is another package that provides advanced text processing tools, such as n-gram and collo-
cation extraction, pattern matching, and topic modeling. Here
is an example of how to use the quanteda package to extract
collocations from text data:

```
library(quanteda)
# load text data
text_data <- "This␣is␣an␣example␣sentence.␣Here␣is␣another␣
    example␣sentence."

# tokenize text
text_tokens <- tokens(text_data)

# extract collocations
collocations <- text_tokens %>%
tokens_ngrams(n = 2) %>%
textstat_collocations()
```

The stm package is a package that provides tools for topic modeling, which is a technique for uncovering hidden themes or
topics in a collection of documents. The stm package offers
functions for preprocessing text data, estimating topic models,
and visualizing the results. Here is an example of how to use
the stm package to estimate a topic model:

```
library(stm)
# load text data
text_data <- data.frame(text = c("This␣is␣a␣sentence␣about␣
    topic␣1", "This␣is␣a␣sentence␣about␣topic␣2", "This␣is␣
    a␣sentence␣about␣topic␣3"))

# preprocess text
text_data <- textProcessor(text_data$text, language = "
    english")
prep_documents <- prepDocuments(text_data$documents,
    text_data$vocab, lower.thresh = 3)
```

```
# estimate topic model
```

6.18   Describe the use of R in the development of advanced techniques for data integration, data cleaning, and data transformation.

R has many powerful packages for data integration, data cleaning, and data transformation. Some of the most commonly used packages for these tasks include tidyr, dplyr, reshape2, data.table, and plyr.

tidyr is a package for data tidying, which involves transforming datasets to a more consistent and standardized format. The package provides functions such as gather() and spread() for converting between wide and long formats, and separate() and unite() for splitting and combining variables.

dplyr is a package for data manipulation, which involves filtering, sorting, grouping, and summarizing data. The package provides functions such as filter(), arrange(), group_by(), and summarize() for these tasks, and uses a "grammar of data manipulation" syntax that is easy to read and write.

reshape2 is a package for data reshaping, which involves changing the layout of datasets. The package provides functions such as melt() and cast() for converting between wide and long formats, and can be useful for tasks such as reshaping survey data or time series data.

data.table is a package for data manipulation that is optimized for large datasets. It provides a fast and memory-efficient implementation of the "data.table" data structure, which can perform operations like filtering, sorting, and grouping on very large datasets with minimal memory usage.

plyr is a package for data manipulation and transformation that provides functions like ddply() and ldply() for splitting and combining data frames, and join() for merging data frames.

In addition to these packages, R has many other packages that can be used for data integration, data cleaning, and data transformation, depending on the specific needs of a project. Some examples of these packages include stringr for string manipulation, forcats for factor manipulation, and janitor for data cleaning.

Overall, R's extensive collection of packages for data manipulation and transformation makes it a powerful tool for cleaning and preparing data for analysis.

6.19 Discuss the role of R in the development of cutting-edge techniques for data privacy and security, such as differential privacy and secure multiparty computation.

R has emerged as one of the leading programming languages for data science and statistical analysis, and its role is expanding to address new challenges related to data privacy and security. In recent years, there has been growing interest in developing advanced techniques for data privacy and security that can provide robust protection for sensitive information while enabling effective data analysis and modeling.

One key approach to data privacy is differential privacy, which is a framework for analyzing data that provides strong guarantees of privacy protection while preserving statistical accuracy. R has several packages that enable the implementation of differential privacy, including the dp package, which provides tools for computing differentially private statistics and queries, and the diffpriv package, which provides functions for generating differentially private synthetic data.

Another important area of research in data privacy and security is secure multi-party computation (SMPC), which allows multiple parties to compute on a shared dataset without revealing any sensitive information. R has several packages that enable the implementation of SMPC, including the smpc package, which provides tools for performing basic arithmetic and logic operations on shared data, and the PrivateRM package, which provides tools for performing linear regression using secure multi-party computation.

In addition to these specific techniques, R also offers a range of tools and libraries for data encryption, hashing, and secure data transmission. For example, the openssl package provides functions for encryption and decryption using the OpenSSL library, while the digest package provides functions for computing hash values of data. The httr package offers support for secure HTTP communication using SSL/TLS encryption.

Overall, R is playing an increasingly important role in the development of advanced techniques for data privacy and security, as well as in the broader landscape of data science and statistical programming languages. Its rich ecosystem of packages and libraries enables researchers and practitioners to address a wide range of challenges related to data privacy and security, and to develop new and innovative approaches to these important issues.

6.20 Explain the use of R in the development of advanced tools and platforms for data education, data literacy, and data communication.

R is a powerful and flexible statistical programming language that is widely used for data analysis, modeling, and visualization. Its versatility has made it an ideal choice for developing advanced tools and platforms for data education, data literacy, and data communication.

One of the main strengths of R is its ability to create interactive and engaging data visualizations that help users better understand complex data sets. There are many packages available in R that allow users to create interactive graphics, such as ggplot2, plotly, and Shiny. For example, the ggplot2 package provides a powerful and flexible system for creating publication-quality graphics, while plotly allows users to create interactive plots and dashboards that can be shared online.

In addition to its powerful graphics capabilities, R is also well-suited for developing tools and platforms for data education and data literacy. For example, the swirl package provides a platform for interactive R tutorials that teach users the basics of programming in R. The package allows users to work through a series of interactive lessons that cover topics such as data manipulation, data visualization, and statistical analysis.

Another package, called datacamp, provides a platform for interactive online courses in data science and programming. The platform offers a wide range of courses in topics such as data manipulation, data visualization, and machine learning, and provides users with interactive exercises and quizzes to help reinforce their learning.

R is also well-suited for developing tools and platforms for data communication. For example, the knitr package allows users to create dynamic reports that combine text, code, and graphics. These reports can be exported in a variety of formats, including HTML, PDF, and Microsoft Word. This allows users to easily create and share dynamic reports that provide insights into complex data sets.

Overall, the flexibility and power of R make it an ideal choice for developing advanced tools and platforms for data education, data literacy, and data communication. Its versatility allows it to be used in a wide range of applications, from interactive tutorials to dynamic reports and online courses, making it an essential tool for anyone working with data.

www.ingramcontent.com/pod-product-compliance
Lightning Source LLC
LaVergne TN
LVHW051329050326
832903LV00031B/3443